D1036964

CRITICAL ENCOUNTERS

CRITICAL ENCOUNTERS
Literary Views and Reviews, 1953-1977

by

Nona Balakian

THE BOBBS-MERRILL COMPANY, INC.

Indianapolis/New York

Library of Congress Cataloging in Publication Data

Balakian, Nona.
Critical encounters.

1. Fiction—History and criticism—Collected works. I. Title.

PN3324.B3	1978	823'.9'1409	77-15421
		ISBN 0-672-52341-8	

To my sister Anna

Acknowledgments

The author wishes to gratefully acknowledge the following
sources for permission to reprint:

"On the Reading of Modern Fiction" (originally published in a foreshortened version);
"Affirmation and Love in T. S. Eliot"; "Shaw and His Boswell"; "Reviews by Trill-
ing"; "Criticism Par Excellence: V. S. Pritchett"; "Spearhead of British Modernism";
"A Passion for Letters: Scofield Thayer and the *Dial*"; and "Britain's Lopsided
View." Reprinted with permission from the *New Leader*, 1953-1965, copyright © The
American Labor Conference on International Affairs, Inc.

"The Prophetic Vogue of the Anti-Heroine" reprinted with permission from *Southwest
Review*, Spring 1962.

"Crisis—In Fiction or in Readership?" reprinted with permission from *Barnard Alum-
nae Magazine*, Fall 1965.

"The New Transcendentalists: A Quasi-Religious Mode in American Fiction" reprinted
with permission from *Ararat*, Spring 1967.

"Unwilling Ironists" was originally published in the *Kenyon Review*, Spring 1962.

"Three Post-Psychological Novels" was originally published in the *Kenyon Review*,
Autumn 1958.

"Crossing the Ethnic Barrier" reprinted with permission from *Ararat*, Fall 1968.

"The Decline of 'Mass Markets' " (originally titled "Writers and Their Audiences")
reprinted with permission from *P.E.N. Quarterly*, Spring 1973.

"The Lowly State of Book Reviewing" was originally published as "Journalism's Step-
children: The Book Editors." Reprinted from the *Columbia Journalism Review*,
Winter 1967-68.

Contents

PART THREE

PART FOUR

Introduction

A collection of retrospective essays and reviews with no apparent link must seem an exercise in self-indulgence. And, indeed, midstream, I nearly retracted. To complicate matters, there was my reluctance to exhume past work: life's adventure for me consists in looking ahead and moving on. If nonetheless this volume has materialized, it is because in looking back I see a dimension of interest *outside* the work itself.

For twenty-five years or more, I realize, I have rather deliberately and single-mindedly steered a course through the precarious shoals of literary journalism. The book review's ambiguous position, in newspapers especially, has always made it seem a "lost cause," its presence there a token concession to a special reader interest from which (until recently) hardly any revenue could derive. Yet its challenge—to bring together the ephemeral and the enduring—has remained intact and continues to involve me today with the same kind of excitement I felt when, fresh out of Graduate School, I resolved to use journalism for literary ends. To divert readers from the frozen reality of everyday facts calls for a sinuous and cajoling skill alien to a purer form of criticism. But because of the immediacy of its impact, book reviewing has another kind of importance: its social reverberations, its potential for influencing currents of thought and modes of taste and action are, if at all acknowledged, greatly undervalued. In a modest way this volume affirms my own commitment to its larger possibilities as a craft and a vocation.

Literary journalism in its many guises has been on the American scene for a very long time. At its peak in the 1920s and 1930s, it churned up many of our eminent literary critics. Before he became a noted author, Edmund Wilson was book critic of the *New Republic;* later, in the 1940s, he wielded great influence over the course of contemporary letters through his book review columns in the *New Yorker.* It was in the pages of another magazine, the *Dial,* that T. S. Eliot developed his views of poetic drama, that Ezra Pound "discovered" William Carlos Williams. Writing for a more general audience, Clifton Fadiman, Alfred Kazin, Stanley Edgar Hyman, Orville Prescott and Charles Poore devoted lifetimes to evaluating literature as it came off the press. Book reviewers in the daily or Sunday press have commanded power second only to that of critics who traditionally cluster around university-sponsored literary quarterlies. Today, with the receding influence of the "little magazines" (which have grown increasingly specialized), the book page or book supplement has acquired a potential for unlimited authority over the public's literary taste.

This was hardly the situation when I entered the field in the mid-1940s. Like most young people involved in their own aspirations, I was hardly aware of the changes waiting in the wings for the "profession." It had all begun so propitiously for me. As an apprentice reviewer on the staff of the *New York Times Book Review,* I was asked to review, in quick succession, a critical study of Hawthorne, the collected works of O. Henry, and a narrative poem of Oliver La Farge. When these reviews were published under my byline, I felt vindicated before my English professors, who had frowned on my turning to journalism as a career. In their view, not only would I blunt my literary sensibilities by writing for the press, but I would forever block my creative propensities. Not that I renounced overnight the hope they held out to me of becoming a playwright (in the Chekhovian vein!), but journalism's promise of a more immediate communication with the world proved more enticing just then.

We were not "activists" in those days (the term had not been invented), but as the first generation to know the meaning of total war, we were very much aware of a world "out there" toward which we felt a personal commitment. Literature was the alchemy through which we hoped to transform the world. As a book reviewer, I would not simply "serve" the public; I would charge others with my enthusiasm for literary art and "smuggle" in, where I could, some ideas of my own about a changing world that contemporary literature, like contemporary art, was quick to absorb and expose.

I was not astute enough at the time to realize that the two journalists who initially took me under their wings were not only extraordinarily gifted men, but in many ways untypical of their profession, and therefore innovative. John Chamberlain, the daily book reviewer of the *New York Times* who had recommended me to the *Book Review* while I was still his student at the Columbia Graduate School of Journalism, dazzled readers with his brilliance and versatility; indeed, no one on that paper before or since has matched his record as a reviewer who combined social, political, historical and literary perspectives in almost equal measure. The shifts in his political convictions in a transitional period were born of an analytical pragmatism and scrupulous soul-searching; they were in striking contrast to the straitjacketed mind that had so recently threatened the world. A review by John Chamberlain was not simply about a book, it was oneself confronting that book: reading him, one found out just where one stood.

As an editor, Robert van Gelder, who had just taken charge of the *Book Review* when I came on the scene, was a maverick with ideas of his own. In 1943, van Gelder, a relatively young general assignment reporter and book reviewer, was invited to succeed the influential editor-essayist J. Donald Adams. Himself literature oriented, van Gelder saw the *Book Review* as an educative medium. Since the supplement is indirectly dependent on advertising (it determines the size of the *Review*), he couldn't ignore popular books of the day, particularly novels, from which the bulk of the advertising derives, but the reviews he printed of these books invariably exposed what was irrelevant or false or blatantly commercial about them. He had a knack for finding young writers with literary backgrounds and the necessary gift for performing total surgery on crass products. William Du Bois, a staff reviewer, was an incredibly facile and inspired wrecker of bad novels, and I began by wanting to emulate him. Alas, I proved no match. My own inclination, it turned out, lay in the opposite direction: building up ambitious noncommercial literary work. I invariably gathered around me (and still do to this day) writers whose gifts were not directly attuned to the prevailing "market." It was the avant-garde writers, short-story practitioners, belletrists and foreign writers (appearing in translation for the first time) who found a sympathetic ear in me.

Under van Gelder, I was encouraged to search out the literary/academic university press books (until then hardly considered "reviewable"), both to review myself and to assign to others. Van Gelder allowed me, an inexperienced young writer, to inject my ideas and reflections in reviews when they helped elucidate the meaning of the book at hand or provided a useful frame of reference. In the two years of his editorship, van Gelder drew to the *Review* many eminent writers, as well as some who were on their way up. He responded to individuality in writing and knew how to profit from what was unique in a writer's experience and background. Eudora Welty, whom he invited to be on the staff during the brief period she lived in New York, wrote many brilliant reviews, some under different pseudonyms, since she would often write more than one review for an issue. Others who wrote for him with some regularity were Marguerite Young (then best known as a poet), F. O. Matthiessen, R. L. Duffus (the *Times*'s own eloquent editorial writer), Prof. Robert Gorham Davis (who continued to review with distinction for three decades), Howard Mumford Jones and Lionel Trilling. Younger unknowns like Nash Burger, Tom Lask and myself were allowed now and then to compete with "name" reviewers in the front part of the *Review*. Van Gelder's own weekly interviews with authors were among the best that the paper has ever printed, because they captured the writer in his totality.

But if I was inspired by Chamberlain's and van Gelder's examples, I found it hard to break free of the hack work that inevitably became the lot of the staff reviewer. In the days before the "specialists" took over, it was not unusual for staff reviewers to write two or three reviews each week. To offset the tedium of writing about the run-of-the-mill fiction I was assigned, I devised a style of pithy criticism that would relate to reader and writer alike. Looking back, I see that I was not exactly humble in my mission to "improve" current literature while at the same time "guiding" current taste, and the mail that came to mean the most to me was from authors who claimed to have profited from my comments.

All along I was nudging my editors (who had a way of changing with some regularity at this point) to assign more literary books to scholarly reviewers, and I offered to review some which I felt qualified to handle. In the short time that he was editor, John K. Hutchens, who subsequently became daily book reviewer for the *Herald-Tribune*, bolstered my wishes along this line and generally expanded the coverage of literary titles.

In those pre-women's lib days, no one (least of all myself) drew attention to the fact that I was the only woman on the staff (then numbering ten, all told) dealing with adult books. I thought it a mere coincidence—like the fact that I appeared to be the only person (male or female) who knew enough French to be able to interview François Mauriac. When I filed my "story" from Aise-et-Oise (outside Paris), where the novelist received me with much fanfare, I felt that I had at last "arrived" as a literary journalist.

Thereafter I became a candidate for all those inevitable fringe benefits: invitations to write for other sections of the paper and for other publications; to lecture; to attend dinner parties, where one is flanked by best-selling authors and young hopefuls; to meet for business lunches at Sardi's and the Algonquin, where, between mouthfuls of gourmet dishes, publicists ply you with their lists of Big Books. (Somehow I always come away more interested in the publicists themselves than in their wares.)

The postwar boom in readership had made publishing a profitable enterprise, but it was not yet big business. It attracted individualists who wanted to leave their mark on the culture. Among these were the refugee publishers from Europe: the brilliant couple Kurt and Helen Wolff from Munich (who founded Pantheon Books), the energetic and gracious team of Marian and Hanna Kister from Warsaw (Mrs. Kister still runs the firm of Roy). Slightly bewildered by their new surroundings, they were full of fervor about introducing the new voices that wartime Europe had produced. Being in their company added an important dimension to my literary education. On the publishing scene, all was hope and progress: to all appearances, a convivial personal relationship existed among writers, editors and publishers. At the *Times* office, literature arrived at one's feet by the crateful each day. It was easy to move with the tide.

The editors of the *Times*'s editorial page in those days (first Charles Merz, then John B. Oakes) maintained a close relationship with the *Book Review* staff and sought contributions from it on cultural subjects. Nobody (including the music editor) had thought of honoring Chopin's anniversary, so I pitched in as a Chopin buff! I blush to think that they published *all* that I wrote—luckily unsigned. If I wanted to draw attention to anything dealing with books or writers—the new National Book Awards, a Nobel Prize winner, a publisher who deserved praise or chiding—I had only to ask: writing an unsigned editorial, where no personal modesty need enter, provided a heady kind of exhilaration, a feeling of being in full command that I had still to sense as a critic.

Beyond and above all, there was a continuous opportunity to meet writers, old and new, often leading to permanent friendships: Saul Bellow, when he had published his first book, *Dangling Man*—shy, intense, ascetic-looking; Eudora Welty, soon after the publication of her second book of stories—full of the joy of life, as she remains to this day (one of our great writers and a cherished friend); Carson McCullers, in deep pain in her last years, but warm-hearted and eager to communicate when interviewed in her Nyack home; the critic V. S. Pritchett (another writer I had the privilege of interviewing), whose regular "London Literary Letters" were the high points of my copyreading chores; the unchanging, buoyant William Saroyan, who would breeze in (as he still does) from Fresno or Paris, stirring up my Armenian soul; the dazzlingly beautiful Anaïs Nin in her sixties, handing me the first volume of her *Diary* in manuscript, trembling to know if I thought it would at last bring her to the larger public's attention; a genial, gentle Kurt Vonnegut, relishing a Saroyan play with me and a band of Saroyan fans. Through my association with these and lesser known writers, I was discovering my own inner resources and my particular concerns as a writer. Every day at the *Times* I was witnessing the first hesitant steps of a new literature. To discover writers in the 1950s was an easy thing to do; they were standing in the wings, ready to explode.

In the early 1950s the *Book Review* underwent a major metamorphosis. Just as I was beginning to think I had become skilled in writing under pressure of a deadline, reviewing by the staff virtually ceased. In a trend that continues to this day, the emphasis shifted from the book as an entity to the topic covered in it. Not that excellence was overlooked, but timeliness and general interest became extra measures of a book's current worth and important factors in determining the extent of its visibility in the *Review.* Experts were now sought to deal with subjects hitherto passed up as being too specialized (scientific, military, sociological, etc.); even fiction was viewed in terms of its general subject matter and/or locale and assigned accordingly to reviewers familiar with one or the other. (Thus, a novel about the South would be assigned to a Southern writer, a novel about Hollywood to a writer who had worked on movie scripts, and so on.)

The new editor, Francis Brown (who remained in the post until 1970), was a seasoned journalist, having served on three major publications—*Current History,* the *New York Times Magazine* and *Time*—and had also taught briefly at Columbia. All these connections proved invaluable to him in finding specialists for books on current events. Brown increasingly depended on me to ferret out writers with specialties in literature who could be counted on to write for a general readership. The combination of scholar-writer has never been an easy one to find, but because there were still a number of literary magazines around and academics had relatively more leisure then, Brown's roster of reviewers soon grew into a Who's Who of contemporary literature: it seemed for a while that books were being written in order to establish their writers' credentials to review for *TBR!*

With so many part-time reviewers around, the professional reviewer fell on hard times. In my own case, the situation proved providential. I had become restless, wanting to extend my range, explore new fields and possibly move on to a more scholarly level of criticism. But here there were hurdles to be met. As a nonacademic, I felt automatically excluded from certain quarterlies; being nonpolitical, I remained an "outsider" with relation to others; and as a *Times* byliner, I was ineligible to become a regular contributor to magazines like *Harper's* and *Saturday Review.*

Through my scholar/critic sister (Anna Balakian), I began to be drawn to an academic world that had a vital, contemporary ambiance. There was nothing cold and formal, and scarcely anything forbiddingly technical, in the area of modern literature and poetry that Anna had made her own. The author of a book (her first) that introduced literary surrealism in this country, she dealt with a subject that was ruled by strong creative impulses. Criticism, as she and some of her colleagues practiced it, was a continuous search for new illuminations. This approach gave a creative edge to reviewing, and it threw into focus for me much of the new writing that had appeared unintelligible.

Fitfully, I resumed the freelance reviewing I had done earlier for Eileen Garrett's *Tomorrow,* a quirky, offbeat magazine that occasionally delved into the occult (the editor's special interest) but was down-to-earth in its book-review section, where unknown young writers were encouraged to air their literary views. In the 1950s I found myself drawn to a weekly magazine that combined news with opinions on a variety of cultural and political topics. Politically left of right, the *New Leader,* edited by S. M. Levitas, was cordial to *Times* writers, many of whom were encouraged to write opinionated reviews.

Introduction

The excellence of the *New Leader's* book section in those years reflected the wide interests of its literate and enthusiastic book-review editor, Mary Greene. A warm and attractive personality, she had a gift for drawing out the particular enthusiasms of a writer. Having printed my article "On the Reading of Modern Fiction" and my interview with V. S. Pritchett, she would call on me at regular intervals to suggest books for me to review or to ask for some suggestions from me. If fewer people read my reviews in the *New Leader*, there was a compensating factor in the knowledge that they were being read by a specialized audience. It was gratifying, too, to be able to choose my books and thereby develop certain areas of expertise. It was Mary Greene who suggested that I review T. S. Eliot's *The Elder Statesman,* aware as she was of my interest in Eliot as a playwright. Knowing it was an uneven play, I hedged at first. But I am glad I accepted the assignment, for the review brought me my most prized fan letter—from T. S. Eliot himself.

It is to Lionel Trilling that I owe my stint as a book reviewer for the *Kenyon Review* (now defunct, alas) and my subsequent branching out into other publications. Trilling, whom I knew slightly, was the critic I most admired in those years, and his influence was one that I felt strongly. I was infinitely grateful to be noticed by him and to have him recommend me to the editor of the *Kenyon Review,* John Crowe Ransom. It was not only prestigious but "chic" at that time to write for a magazine that favored the New Criticism. Though the style was familiar to me, I made no conscious effort to assimilate it. Yet I felt at home in the kind of close textual analysis the New Critics championed. Perhaps my background in French literature and my strict training in *explication du texte* had given me the proper preparation.

My inclination has always been to define as precisely as possible what I see as the distinctive quality of a particular writer; in fiction, especially, I am curious to know the *how* that follows the *what:* by what means has the writer succeeded (or failed) in doing what he does? That *how* depends a great deal on technique in the broadest sense of the term, namely form and style. Mark Schorer's "Technique as

Discovery" was an essay that greatly impressed me when it appeared, and to this day I hold myself back whenever I find I have placed too great an emphasis on content apart from the form in which a serious work of fiction has its true meaning.

Writing in magazines, I not only was able to examine individual writers and separate books, but could attempt evaluations of writers in a group (e.g., The Angry Young Men) or analyze and pinpoint the climate of the contemporary scene. It was inevitable that I should be drawn to the "new" American writers whose careers had begun soon after World War II and who by the end of the 1950s had accumulated an impressive body of work. Under the pressure of deadline, book reviewers generally handle a writer's books singly as they are published and thus often fail to convey the sum total of his style and accomplishment. For the same reason, they cannot readily perceive what contemporaries have in common. But there was an additional reason why, as late as the end of the 1950s, the postwar writers had remained invisible both as separate voices and as a group with a certain common vision. Because these writers were turning away from established styles of realism, the elder critics then in power were unwilling or unable to accept their innovations. The face of contemporary American fiction has changed so drastically in the past sixteen years that it is hard to believe that in 1961, when I proposed an anthology of critical essays on postwar American writers like Bellow, Mailer, Welty, Updike and Nabokov, it was readily accepted by a major publisher. Doubleday, in fact, seized on it as a necessary text for making these writers better understood by the general public.

As I pointed out in my introduction to *The Creative Present: Notes on Contemporary American Fiction,* the need for such a volume arose because no contemporary literary historian was doing for these writers what Malcolm Cowley had done for an earlier group of moderns. My collaborator Charles Simmons and I made our selection of seventeen writers after much soul-searching, and proceeded to look for the ideal author-critic matches. As editors of the *Book Review,* we were not new to the task, except that in this instance it was important to find critics who could write from a broad base of engagement with the entire oeuvre of their subject. No doubt the sensitive and intelligent articles we were able to obtain from various prominent critics partly reflected on our own close engagement with these writers.

I like to think that my brush with literary criticism in a variety of magazines has had a salutary effect on my book reviewing, which I still continue to do for the daily *Times* and elsewhere, while remaining on the *Book Review* as an editor. It was Christopher Lehmann-Haupt who initially created the opportunity for me to review for the daily *Times* when he asked me to substitute for him while he was on vacation. Chris, who is a reviewer of enviable broad background and interests, did not mind that I would be giving scant attention to topical books: he knew that even if I confined myself to literary titles, I would find books which had some inner (if not surface) relevance to a general readership. As a woman reviewing in the daily *Times* (I believe I was the first), I was naturally tempted to handle books on feminist subjects, which were becoming popular in the early 1960s. One such assignment I set myself was to comment on three anthologies of women poets in a review I titled "Realists of the Interior." I wanted to see whether certain generalizations about women poets were valid. But when I found out what these poets indeed had in common, I realized that the quest in itself did not really interest me; what mattered in the individual talent had no direct bearing on the group experience.

Some years before women's lib became a force, I also broached the subject of women from another angle. My interest in examining the changing concepts of women in contemporary literature led to my article in *Southwest Review*, "The Prophetic Vogue of the Anti-Heroine." In that instance I did not throw a wide enough net, and I discovered that the real creators of anti-heroines were *men*.

Generally, I have written about women writers (Welty, McCullers, Sarraute, Compton-Burnett, etc.) only out of interest in their separate artistic visions. Sometimes, though, I have written about a woman writer because she has been unfairly ignored by men critics or has not been taken seriously enough by them—and has been slighted by feminist critics as "irrelevant." The writers I have gravitated toward—whether men or women—have been those who involve themselves with life at the profoundest level. I have been fascinated by their views of human nature and behavior, by their new and original ways of revealing these to us, and by the evidence in their work of what Lionel Trilling has called "the moral imagination."

I have also been drawn to writers who conduct a continuous rebellion with the world—not in an overt and violent sense, but internally, and against a general tide that seeks to crush the individual soul. Dissent *has* to be the burden of the idealist in search of a perfect world. True, writers like Beckett and Vonnegut can raise dissent to such an ominous level that cynicism becomes, perversely, a positive value, the only remaining weapon left to an intelligent person. But more generally, the nihilism of current writers is self-defeating, invalidating the very need for art and literature: indeed, it precludes their being achieved, in my view. The creative urge is entwined with transcendence, and affirmation is the eventual goal of both.

Affirmation—not mere assent (which is really a form of accommodation). The affirmative stance comes slowly, often painfully; beginning in self-doubt, it moves on to hopelessness or loss of direction ("In the middle of the journey of our life I came to myself in a dark wood . . ."—Dante); but through harsh self-confrontation comes a reversal, a clearing, a lucidity, sometimes a conversion. Affirmation is awareness that the person matters, that if life does not always add up, it at least has the potential for doing so.

I make these categorical and summary statements not to validate my choice of writers (obviously, there was an element of fortuity in my selection—a book newly published and made available to me at a certain time) but to explain my predilections to readers of this volume. Through all the years that I have reviewed books, I have been fascinated by this polarity of dissent and affirmation, noting their dual presence in writers as various as T. S. Eliot (who moved from disillusionment to religious conversion), Saroyan (who, like the three wise men, was guided by a star visible only to the pure in heart), Shaw

24

and Huxley (who in their separate ways connected the absence of goodness with a failure of intelligence that could in time be reversed), and Salinger (in whom dissent and affirmation become crazily enmeshed, a form of modern madness that I find endlessly provocative in his work).

If literary journalism has confined me to contemporary writing, it has rewarded me with a sense of progression and innovation in art; it has brought me closer to a recognition of a fluid, changing reality, without, I hope, destroying my sense of history; and it has allowed me to straddle the worlds of the creative and the factual mind. In the fusion of my activities as reviewer, essayist and editor, I have been able to view the literary and publishing communities from a variety of perspectives, relating in some degree to all.

I have been continuously concerned about the relationship of writers to their audiences and have voiced my dissatisfaction (in articles and panel discussions) with the tendency to confuse commercial and literary aims. Like Robert van Gelder, I have valued young reviewers for their disinterestedness and fresh viewpoints, wishing I had greater influence in advancing their growth as critics before they surrendered to the demands of the "marketplace." I view the proliferation of the small presses in the 1970s as a sign of health in an era of impersonal conglomerate publishing, but I am wary of the relaxing of standards of professionalism in one-man operations.

Finally, I feel deeply committed to the extension of literary journalism in the country as a whole. At a time when the highest degree of professionalism is being upheld in every field, book reviewers are increasingly being held back, their development blocked by lack of opportunities as newspapers withdraw reviewing space. In the absence of trained generalists, we have a transient band of reviewers who momentarily flash on the scene and as suddenly vanish. However able and ambitious these freelancers may be, they are naturally casual in their commitment to a vocation whose rewards remain generally meager and spotty. Yet the responsibility is a grave one. In the end, it is reviewers who influence the kind of books that get published and the quality of the literature we subsequently develop. If modern literature has not fulfilled the promise it held for us in the 1950s, it may well be because literary journalists have not been sufficiently involved in its fate in recent years.

Nona Balakian
New York City

PART ONE

On the Reading of Modern Fiction

"There is not a critic alive now who will say that the novel is a work of art and that as such he will judge it." Virginia Woolf's lament in her 1927 essay, "The Art of Fiction," bears raising again today* when the status of fiction is conspicuously on the decline. Mass-produced and pampered by publicity, the novel or short story is probably more widely read than ever before. Yet, in contrast to its sister arts of painting, music and poetry, it is still generally treated as the foster child of criticism. Arbitrarily thrown together in some remote corner of the Sunday literary supplement, fiction reviews rarely achieve more than a summary of plot, and when occasionally more than four hundred words are allotted, the space is squandered on irrelevant references to the writer's character, his morals or his politics, with barely a concluding word about how the novel in question has been put together. The more learned reviews in the little magazines, on the other hand, too often turn into knowing essays on what current fiction reveals about the culture of our time.

All well and good. But what happens to the art of fiction? Can we afford to ignore it or claim that it doesn't exist?

Though more than a quarter of a century has passed since the Spanish critic Ortega y Gasset** announced with characteristic

---

*This essay, published in 1954, reflects my dissatisfaction with the generally negative attitude of the critics of the day toward the new generation of postmoderns.

**Cf. *Notes on the Novel,* 1925.

pessimism that the novel had entered its last phase (for lack of subjects to treat), literary prophets still persist in taking up the cry. Now and again they shake their heads sadly at the unpleasantness of its subject matter, its lack of uplift and moral passion. Even more than at its decadence, they rail at its formlessness—presumably the absence of a beginning, a middle and an end. One English critic recently went so far as to attribute the decline of fiction to the neglect of the precept "Proper thoughts in proper order." In sum, it has become a fashionable current of criticism to accuse the literary novel or short story (particularly where it lacks an obvious "social" message) of coating its essential emptiness with a false veneer of "difficult" meaning.

Granting for argument's sake that the English critic was right—that a novelist's meaning should be transparently clear—what are we to say about Proust and Virginia Woolf, about Joyce and Faulkner and all those other masters of the modern novel who have preferred to follow the reverse of "Proper thoughts in proper order"? And how are we to account for the growing number of American writers who are following in their path even at the risk of having their work misunderstood?

To speak of current fiction in terms of "clarity" and "obscurity" is to miss the fact that these are, after all, subjective terms, indicating the relative degree of receptiveness, sympathy and understanding we bring as readers to a work of art. What is within the grasp of our experience is clear; what is alien to it is obscure. It was inevitable that in searching for new ways to convey the new things they had to say, writers would at first confuse the untrained reader. What was less predictable, perhaps, was that they would also confuse a large segment of the critics—those who cannot accept innovation because they will not let the old yardsticks go.

Anything new is necessarily a mental challenge, and modern fiction—the literature of the past sixty or seventy years—by its very nature encourages resistance. Though its roots are in the nineteenth century, it long ago anticipated the world in which we live and is today more contemporary than most of us can be, conditioned as we are by earlier modes of being and of thought. At its best the modern novel has become a kind of fluoroscope—an x-ray eye which probes through the surface of reality to give us glimpses of complex patterns in the very process of taking shape and fixing our lives. To hold the mirror up to nature—a nature which all agreed upon—presented a small challenge as compared to the modern writer's task of piercing through the visible to discover what is secret and hidden and still unsystematized. The novelist with the fluoroscopic eye is necessarily at a disadvantage before the obdurate reader who has always associated reality with the concept of mirrors, of direct and static reflection.

Despite the enormous attraction which the method of naturalism has held periodically for American writers since the beginning of the century, American fiction has not escaped the clear, consistent trend away from the representational realism popularized by the Victorian novel and dignified into a theory of art by Zola and his followers. Long before the end of the century, it had grown familiar with the new sophistication in literature, the new skepticism toward established literary concepts, including that of a standard "human nature." If Dostoevsky and Hardy across the sea had cast an ambiguous light on "good" and "evil," Melville and Hawthorne in this country had launched the counterrealistic tradition that paved the way for the novels of Henry James and the new aesthetics of fiction.

Directly or indirectly, the writer, the artist, began to feel the impact of those daring explorers of our time: the philosopher-scientists. Freud, Bergson and William James, among others, were opening new vistas to human consciousness and discovering dimensions of reality only tentatively imagined until then. The old metaphysics based on belief in absolutes could not but lose ground in a world where "to exist was to change," where a new philosophy of dynamic living revealed the complexity of modern life and, more significant still, the complexity of truth.

At its worst, the result was a total denial of values and, in terms of art in general, a loss of the personal viewpoint, of style. But, at its best, the challenge was met with a new, scrupulous determination to get at the core of things, to discover the very mechanism by which things—and even men and women—become what they are. The basic creative urge which seeks to delve beyond the borders of the finite could only grow keener and more refined through this new explorative tendency of the artist's mind.

Borrowing from modern science not its methods but its philosophy, the new art sought to free itself of postulates and a priori reasoning. It balked at the naturalistic practice of carrying cause and effect to their ultimate conclusion, because to do so was again to assume a predictable human nature. The horror in a story like Thomas Mann's "Mario and the Magician" lies in the suggestion not only that evil is innate but that such evil ultimately finds an echo in its surroundings and so begins to spread its poison. In emphasizing the impact of character on environment, Mann completely reversed the naturalist's intent and achieved a story whose "social" meaning is deep if unobvious.

There were other striking departures for the modern novelist. Bringing no established code of ethics to his work but only a limitless curiosity, he could dispense with such considerations as "indecency" or "unpleasantness" in the choice of subject matter. To satisfy his all-consuming desire to see life "whole" and in its various aspects, he was willing to remain detached, uncommitted to pet theories or principles. There is a marvelous sense of release in Gide's words from his preface to *The Immoralist:* "I have not tried to prove anything but only to paint my picture well and set it in good light."

In a sense the novel was turning once more to the classical ideal of objectivity—the increasing retreat of the novelist from the scene of action. With this obvious difference: that while the classicist dealt objectively with objectively comprehensible material and traditional values, the modern writer sought to deal objectively with highly subjective material—with states of mind and values that had stood the test of experience. Unlike the classicist, the modernist would try as much as possible to avoid generalizations, but like him, in assimilating content and form, would aim to make his meaning implicit in his subject and its treatment. (It is no mere accident that a writer like Hemingway, who completely rejects the explicit in his work, is so often misunderstood; in mistaking the Hemingway hero for the author or his mouthpiece, readers still miss the tragic essence of the Hemingway story which is rooted in an inverted tenderness.)

This insensitivity to implicit meaning is a major source of difficulty for readers of modern fiction. Having been brought up on the straightforward storytelling method of the Victorians, many readers grow impatient with such innovations as mixed time sequences, the frequent shifting from past to present (so destructive to the element of suspense), the abrupt changes of tone and pace, and most of all the use of symbolism that has not yet become universal. (The Faulkner novel manages to use all of these unorthodox methods at one time.) These devices may very well seem like eccentricities to the uninitiated reader. But not only is the writer who uses them consciously satisfying an aesthetic need; he is striving to render an experience more directly and fully.

Though form has become increasingly important to the novel, the word suggests nothing like the rigid Aristotelian framework to the moderns. "Form" or "technique" to them means nothing superimposed or mechanical, nothing traditional like suspense, climax, dramatic contrast, etc. It is the organic structure of the novel that concerns them—the complete fusing of tone, language and general design of the narrative as it is shaped and shapes the overall meaning of the work. It was the practice of the American and English novel before the end of the last century to consider manner and matter separately (the bulk of current fiction still does) instead of as mutually dependent. But important as the old conventions were, they fell short of the modern writer's intent of conveying the *quality* of an experience—that extra dimension of reality which the cinema was to discover much later.

The idea of the novel as a work of art which could be enjoyed as an isolated experience was still new when Joseph Conrad so cogently expounded it, in 1897, in his preface to *The Nigger of the "Narcissus"*:

> It [the novel] must strenuously aspire to the plasticity of sculpture, to the color of painting and the magic suggestiveness of music—which is the art of arts. And it is only through complete unswerving devotion to the perfect blending of form and substance . . . that an approach can be made to plasticity, to color. . . .

Only nine years earlier, Henry James in the essay "The Art of Fiction" had felt compelled to confirm that the novel is "as free and serious a branch of literature as any other." Which would seem to indicate that for Americans, at least, the high seriousness of the novel had still to be proved. It was in the same essay that James made his prophetic pronouncements on the aesthetics of the novel:

> The novel is a living thing, all one and continuous, like any organism, and in proportion as it lives will it be found, I think, that in each of its parts there is something of each of the other parts.

James's dramatic concept of the novel (stemming from his lifelong devotion to the theater), his concern to "render" rather than narrate, the pains he took "to make a place real not descriptively but by something happening there," attest to the value he placed on the new "technique" of fiction. His brilliant method of indirect narration—his boldness in getting rid of the omniscient author—was perhaps his most important contribution to the novel. His repeated use of an intermediary between author and protagonist (a narrator who at the same time takes part in the action and helps to interpret it for the reader) was more than a neat device: it was essential to his organic concept of the novel. Aware that easy definitions and absolute answers were impossible in life, he sought a wider sympathy, a more catholic insight. If life was to be truthfully translated into fiction, it meant that only relative, subjective viewpoints could be given. In telling his story through the eyes of one of his characters, James was able to make us feel that within the limits of a single consciousness we could not hope for more than an *interpretation* of reality.

The new interest in "the art of fiction" which was consciously launched by James and Conrad has not as yet, at midcentury, effected a change in values. But just as the fervid investigations into reality and the meaning of "human nature" led the writer to search for new methods of dealing with human material, so the new experiments in technique may soon lead him to a new set of values. For it is a curious fact that a shift in emphasis can create a new perspective—a new way of viewing the same basic content—and this in turn can bring about a new synthesis.

The all-seeing, undiscriminating fluoroscope of the moderns has traced to their source the most unpleasant truths about our lives and ourselves and in so doing has tried to give a more searching picture of the condition of man. Dark and hopeless on the surface, it is yet a picture shot through with light by implication. Faulkner's innocent "degenerates," the dislocated sinners of Paul Bowles and Tennessee Williams, the lonely half-adults of Truman Capote, the haunted souls of Eudora Welty, the disenchanted idealists of Lionel Trilling—all belong to a generation that has had to fall back on its own resources, its own half-understood, half-realized self. Out of necessity has come a renewal of interest in the human will; we see it broken down for the first time into all its components, observed and analyzed in both its conscious and its unconscious manifestations.

Is it not a sign of maturity, this scrupulous truthfulness, this searching for the source of evil in man's imperfect relation to a world he has made? One is tempted to predict that a new humanism is emerging, a humanism truer than we have ever known, based on values that are psychologically and spiritually defensible. Occupying the center of the writer's interest this time is not the Man of Reason but the Whole Man as he stands revealed by the combined probings of science and the artist's intuition.

1954

The Prophetic Vogue of the Anti-Heroine

In the senseless hubbub over the Return of Lady Chatterley, which pitted the guardians of morality (i.e., the U.S. Post Office) against the champions of D. H. Lawrence and freedom from censorship, one important reason for the novel's enormous appeal was overlooked. Its success hinged only partly on that commonplace ingredient of best-sellerdom, Sex. Many present-day novelists can match Lawrence in explicitness and are patently more "obscene." Where they fall short of him—and this may explain his recurrent popularity—is in the ability to create a palpably real, full-blooded, wholly alluring heroine. Without being a typically romantic heroine with built-in virtues, Connie Chatterley is a genuine woman, warm, responsive, spontaneous. She is, as Lawrence would have her, universal—but in a fresh, contemporary way that after more than a quarter of a century still seems advanced and "liberated."

The reappearance of Lawrence's womanly heroine points up by contrast the radical changes that heroines in our more serious novels and plays have suffered in the past several decades. Gone with the wind are not only Pollyanna and the romantic ideal but the still more nearly indelible image of the conventionally desirable and vulnerable woman, the Mme. Bovarys, Anna Kareninas, and Jennie Gerhardts. Occupying their place more and more conspicuously are creatures so devoid of feminine charm, sensibility, and passion, so wanting in the accepted signposts of character (honesty, endurance, modesty) that to call them heroines smacks of mockery. They might more reasonably be called anti-heroines, since they are as atypical as the anti-hero, that hardheaded, weak-willed being with a highly developed sense of his limitations who began replacing the conventional hero some time ago.

Like the anti-hero, the anti-heroine is no newcomer to the world of fiction. As the exceptional, unpredictable woman, she has lured readers in a variety of guises, from Shakespeare's Shrew to Moll Flanders, from Becky Sharp to Shaw's superwomen—all borderline cases from today's vantage point, redeemed by a certain piquant charm and single-minded intent. What sets the current anti-heroine apart is that she no longer is the exception but is presented as the norm. Indeed, she need hardly fear competition from bona fide heroines. As the hero's choice (however reluctantly made at times), she has achieved status.

A random sampling of recent American fiction yields such unlikely leading ladies as Nabokov's sub-teen of freakish sophistication, the notorious Lolita; Truman Capote's asexual clown, Holly Golightly; that monster of psychosis, the aging movie star of Tennessee Williams's *Sweet Bird of Youth;* Eudora Welty's unwilling backwoods bride, Bonnie Dee, of *The Ponder Heart;* streamlined Brenda, of Philip Roth's *Goodbye, Columbus,* who meets her lover's cynicism more than halfway; not to mention a long line of what Edmund Fuller has called the "female zombies" of James Jones, Norman Mailer, and Nelson Algren.

Nor is the vogue of the anti-heroine a purely American manifestation. To England's Young Angries, women, when they are not comic or grasping, are timid, wing-clipping squirrels. The French view is still less encouraging: one thinks of Anouilh's terrifying portraits of warped and loveless women and of the chameleonlike, nameless heroines of Nathalie Sarraute who all but dissolve in the course of her novels. Everywhere one hears the echo of Gênet's phrase describing woman: "an emblem forever escaping from her womanliness."

What lies behind this denigration or deflation of women in present-day literature? Is it a passing fancy—an artificial reversal of the die-hard romantic convention? Is it, as Leslie Fiedler, in *Love and Death in the American Novel,* would have us believe, the result of a Freudian aberration in the consciousness of male writers, stemming from moral and psychological confusion? Both claims seem possible, yet the nagging question remains: what of the social reality behind the projected image?

However exaggerated she may sometimes appear, the anti-heroine as she is pictured by the writer is not a total fantasy. The facts that the portrait is so well-rounded and that there are so many variations on a theme suggest that more than caprice or congenital myopia is here involved. In the work of a number of serious writers the new image of the heroine is a conscious projection of some deep-seated dissatisfactions and an honest acceptance of changing concepts of personal relationships.

Women in literature, except in the instances when they have broken a commandment or brought some miracle to pass, have traditionally been subsidiary figures, treated uncritically and seen more often as prototypes than as individuals. Nor has this simply been the fault of misguided male writers. Women themselves, even since they got the vote and became "emancipated," have helped to foster a static concept of their sex. Only with the impact of psychology and coeducation have they slowly cut a wedge in the mold to assert their individuality. It is curious that two male writers have done most in our time to liberate them in fiction; the de-romanticization of women which began with G. B. Shaw and D. H. Lawrence promises at last to come to full fruition.

It was Shaw's contention that of all the untested criteria by which the male animal ruled his life, none was more delusive than his notion of woman as romantic and pliant. In play after play, he showed up his women protagonists for what they were: hardheaded, aggressive, down-to-earth. Whether they come from the lower ranks, like Vivie Warren, or have position and brains, like Candida; whether they wield power, like the young Cleopatra, or are dependent on a benefactor, like Liza Doolittle, they are always unsentimental and in full command of their destiny. It is women, with their awareness of the Life Force, who shatter the dreams of romantic, illusion-ridden men and finally rob them of their impractical freedom. Yet Shaw's women are never disagreeable; they have character, purpose, and a charm (however "unfeminine") that captivates. They are, of course, in every instance the exceptional woman who, newly awakened in her authentic nature, has tapped the sources of her real power.

For D. H. Lawrence, the exceptional woman has another kind of individuality. She is a being released from bondage to conventional patterns of human relationship. In love, she demands a more equal footing with her partner; she is as assertive as he, as jealous of her fulfillment, and as wary of surrendering her deeper self. In *Women in Love* Lawrence pictured the ideal love relationship as "two pure beings balancing each other . . . . in each the individual is primal, sex subordinate, but perfectly polarized. Each has a single, separate being, with its own laws. The man has his pure freedom, the woman hers." Lawrence's composite heroine with her sharp self-awareness, her healthy sensuality, and her insight into "unknown modes of being" was bound to disturb if not immediately extend or change the portrait of the conventional heroine.

However determined they were to look at women with unprejudiced eyes, both Shaw and Lawrence idealized their heroines in the sense that they remained models of possibility, still to be achieved in fact. The writer of today, on the other hand, having the Shaw-Lawrence blueprints before him, is more inclined to face facts and to show us the disparity that exists between what should be and what is. His own attitude is revealed indirectly through his characterizations of women and more directly through his heroes' responses to them.

In the work of J. D. Salinger, for instance, it is significant that there is not a single woman of maturity or stature: there are "dames" to be "had," or there are children, still unspoiled and chastely loving. The exceptional Glass family apart, his "hip" young men, on the surface all prep-school sophistication and know-how, have an inner quality of innocence that is in constant conflict with the codes and mores of their time and place: miniature Hamlets in a world gone awry, they lack the intellectual discipline and hence the comfort of rationalization. (Intellect is bought at too high a price, as Seymour, Buddy, and Zooey Glass demonstrate.) Less adapted to their surroundings than they pretend to be, and only dimly aware (being unanchored in faith) of a spiritual dimension in themselves, these young men feel an instinctive revulsion against the realities of life that at times verges on a rejection of life itself. In this schizophrenic atmosphere of the mind, where the opposing truths of matter and spirit converge, women assume a dualistic aspect of innocence and experience. In the latter category are those who have swallowed whole the phony formulas of "modern living"; though temporarily to be enjoyed, they are ultimately to be renounced.

Possessed of an unconscious urge toward regeneration, Holden Caulfield in *The Catcher in the Rye* and the many young men in *Nine Stories* are drawn to youth in its purest essence. It is no mere accident that in every instance the good angel bears the face of a little girl (or sometimes a nun). For while love redeems, the *capacity* to love, Salinger's young men discover, is dimmed as child grows into woman.

The most striking of these children is Holden's little sister Phoebe, "old Phoebe," to whom he can turn when in trouble, "who always listens when you tell her something and knows half the time what the hell you're talking about." In Phoebe, Salinger demonstrates the power of a love in which there is no possessiveness, only a child's pure commitment and trust. There is Esmé ("To Esmé—With Love and Squalor"), the forthright thirteen-year-old English girl whose affection and concern, because they are gratuitously given, reach across the seas to a lonely, half-deranged American soldier. There is unloved, half-blind Ramona ("Uncle Wiggily in Connecticut") who momentarily, as she sleeps, melts the heart of her hardened suburban mother. And who can forget little Sybil of Salinger's most cryptic story, "A Perfect Day for Bananafish"—Sybil, whose innocent camaraderie briefly comforts a young man on the brink of suicide but fails to save him, because (this is dimly implied) he has suddenly glimpsed through her childish nature the despiritualized, artificial, self-centered woman she is to become? Beneath the wry humor and apparent cynicism of Salinger's stories is a poignant and melancholy understanding of the connection between injured sensibility and alienation from life—from women, who represent life.

Like Salinger's, Truman Capote's taste in women gravitates toward the immature—but for a different reason. His leading ladies are virtually children, but unlike Salinger's they are not necessarily pure. They are, in fact, as in the case of Holly Golightly in *Breakfast at Tiffany's,* so inured to the ways of the world that freedom consists in departing from them. Married at fourteen to an elderly widower with children nearly her own age (out of compassion and in response to his compassion), Holly has subsequently run away to become a "respectable" tramp or "travelling" woman, as she elegantly puts it on her calling card. Of her various talents, her greatest is for spontaneous companionship, which she gives freely to anyone in her immediate vicinity who happens to need it; whether it is a stray cat or a human being, her loyalty is equally engaged. Without exactly falling in love, the narrator becomes curiously attached to Holly: "I was in love with her just as once I'd been in love with my mother's elderly colored cook and a postman who let me follow him on his round, and a whole family named McKendrick." What she inspires is a nonerotic, tender affection which recognizes what is different and unique in another person and ends up strengthening the capacity to love. If Salinger's heroes seek spiritual survival through identification with innocence, Capote's characters appear to seek, in the same unconscious way, to extend their sensibility by embracing "the halt and the blind," the unaffiliated, the outsiders. And the less they hold to accepted patterns of behavior, the more indifferent they are to their "maleness" and "femaleness," the easier it becomes for them to transcend artificial barriers to communication.

"I never think like I'm a girl," says the teen-ager Idabel to her playmate Joel in *Other Voices, Other Rooms.* "You've got to remember that or we can never be friends." This self-assertive, loyal tomboy, whom Joel finds "the maddest of human beings," typifies an attitude of true equality with men which Capote's women reveal. Sufficient unto themselves, they can be truly gratuitous; love does not become an excuse for satisfying the ego's need and so can rise to an almost mystical plane. In the sometimes macabre, sometimes carnival world of Truman Capote, the odd, the grotesque, the sexless and the deviate help to emphasize his essential message: "Love should be allowed in any form. . . . Any love is natural and beautiful that lies in a person's nature."

In total contrast to Capote's undersexed heroines are Tennessee Williams's pathologically oversexed ones. Most of the time sex is the ruling force of their lives, and it renders them pitiful if not always tragic. Not that Williams, a disciple of Lawrence, is remotely a Victorian prude. The crux of his dissatisfaction lies not with sex itself but with its unhealthy thwarting. What the conventional playgoer mainly finds shocking about his plays is the sympathy he brings to his antiheroines. Whether they are lusty "cats," respectable prostitutes, or latent lesbians, they are all hoping to find in their panic-stricken pursuit of desire the universal prize—lost youth and self-identity. "Panic drove me," is how Blanche Du Bois defends her lapse into promiscuity in *A Streetcar Named Desire:* panic to find after the death of her dissolute husband the self she imagined had been caged these many years. But that self, a fabricated image of gentility and innocence, is beyond recall, and the real self, disused and unengaged, has atrophied.

In *The Roman Spring of Mrs. Stone* and in his play *Sweet Bird of Youth,* he has calculatingly chosen as his heroines aging actresses whose days of glory are long past and who seek in sex "the only dependable distraction" from the enemy, time. Motivated solely by greed for success and power (the only way they know of asserting their identity), they face maturity with no inner resources and become pathetic if not grotesque in their efforts to simulate passion. Williams's power-ridden women manage to seduce and dominate the men they lure into their net. But only for a short time. The hard glare of age is merciless on their empty souls and diminishing responses, and they become vulnerable to deception and betrayal.

In his most interesting novel to date, *The Deer Park,* Norman Mailer places a similar emphasis on the misguided sexuality of his oppressed heroines; but because he is something more of a romantic about women than is Williams, he shifts the guilt largely onto male attitudes. Denying God and morality, Mailer's heroes or anti-heroes emerge as inverted rebels committed to no cause outside themselves. Thus Sergius O'Shaugnessy, the boy orphan whom the war has turned into a "hero," analyzes the dissatisfaction he feels: "I didn't know what was right, and I didn't know if I cared, and I didn't even know if I knew what I wanted or what was going on in me."

For an answer, they turn to women as they might turn to an anodyne or to vitamins, expecting to be soothed or renewed and to bolster their waning sense of self. Eitel, the once famous movie director who is desperately trying to make a comeback after being blacklisted, feels at once invigorated in the arms of Elena Esposito, a girl he has taken off a colleague's hands on short notice.

Like most cynics he was profoundly sentimental about sex. It was his dream of bounty, and it nourished him enough to wake up with the hope that this affair could return his energy, flesh his courage, and make him the man he once believed himself to be.

When he tires of this girl, there will be others to fill the bill: it is the response, not the woman, that matters.

Used this way, Elena and her kind are forced into scattering their feelings, shifting their loyalties with a casual promiscuousness that leaves them feeling nothing at all. It is this awareness which makes Elena (Mailer's most successful fallen heroine) suffer with Dostoevskyan intensity and finally face the shocking self-revelation: "You know what the truth is? I never loved anybody in my whole life. Not even myself. I don't know what love is. . . . I'm no good. I'm a prostitute, like everybody else." To the pitiful urgency of her question, "What am I going to do with my life?" Eitel responds simply by fondling her as one would an unhappy child. Not only is he philosophically unequal to helping her; but, unaware of her reality as a fellow being, he is unable to summon up the needed compassion.

In striking contrast to Mailer's almost cloying pity for his heroines is Mary McCarthy's objective view and supercritical treatment of hers. An ironist whose barbs are directed at the confused morality of a fluid society, she delves into the minds of her women characters with savage honesty. Margaret Sargent in *The Company She Keeps* is typical of the new woman with her passion for experimenting with life and for exploring new areas of sensual experience. Poised between reason and impulse, she will not let the new freedom interfere with the illusions she sustains of her moral superiority. Thus she is not averse to being seduced by a lonely elderly man on a night train, but when the experience is over she can forget and rationalize: "She had felt tired and kind and thought, why not?"

A later version of the McCarthy heroine reveals a diminished individualism and self-possession. In the age of conformity, new social pressures complicate the search for self-realization. Like all her suburban contemporaries, Martha Sinnott in *A Charmed Life* is committed to a fixed pattern of marital bliss, a pattern that is threatened when her former husband, Miles Murphy, appears on the scene and makes advances. Foreseeing no consequences, Martha (who is described by her second husband, John, as "an open-minded child") succumbs, and in the clear light of day she can still feel no regret. "She could not believe that having slept with Miles could make any difference to the true reality which was her life with John."

What makes Martha incapable of feeling guilt is that she is a divided being who separates what her body feels from the reality her mind accepts. Nothing she experiences can change her, because nothing leaves a lasting impression. When she discovers that she is to have a child that might be Miles's, she plots an abortion and plans to forget the whole thing like a bad dream. She will have nothing less than the best of both worlds.

If too much calculating intellect atrophies the feelings of Mary McCarthy's heroines, a kind of willed brainlessness achieves a similar effect for heroines of a more recent vintage, the "cool chicks" of Jack Kerouac's world. Wandering, shiftless voluptuaries, they are the new bohemians, dedicated to sex as "the only holy and important thing in life." The old revolt against sexual restrictions is replaced by an anxiety to "make it," to achieve physical communion through an experimental sex. The tension in a novel like *The Subterraneans* centers almost wholly on whether or not the black girl and the white boy will prove sexually (not socially) compatible.

Virtually nameless and faceless, Kerouac's anti-heroines might be reincarnations of Oriental concubines. Preponderantly physical, ever ready to take part in sex orgies in which they are bandied about like playthings, they are yet, like Williams's heroines, curiously passionless in their deliberate pursuit of lust. For sex has become a ritual.

As one of them tellingly remarks in *The Dharma Bums:* "I feel like the mother of all things and have to take care of my little children."

It is hard to know to what extent Kerouac identifies himself with the world of the beats. Is the Zen Buddhist philosophy as they practice it something he accepts at face value, or is it partly at least a convenient device for exposing symptomatic attitudes of our time? One is never quite sure where his criticism of a cliché-ridden society begins and admiration of his "bums" ends.

This is hardly the case with Vladimir Nabokov and his notorious novel *Lolita*. His stand is clear-cut. In the nymphet Lolita he has consolidated a negative view of liberated woman which in effect embraces much of the criticism implied by the other writers discussed. Nabokov's tour de force, the source of the book's real shock, is that he could make us believe in the suffering and ecstasy of a pathological love, could engage our sympathy for the middle-aged Humbert Humbert who is thus afflicted. He was able to do this because he saw that the real aggressor, ironically, was not the abnormal Humbert but the seemingly normal Lolita. Thus, while Humbert languishes in the sweet transport and rapture of love, Lolita cynically and selfishly appropriates Humbert's passion—first in the spirit of voluptuous excitement, later with a design to bargain for material advantages.

Poor Humbert is unable to understand her indifference—"as if [her passion] were something she had sat upon and was too indolent to remove." For Lolita, at thirteen, amorous relations are a commonplace that she must face with boredom: "All that noise about boys gags me," she protests. Used up physically before her deeper feelings have been aroused, she cannot grow to the real meaning of love. Her lust for life has no other object than creature comforts and infantile excitements. As our last glimpse of her suggests, she will grow old before having known what it is to be young and fulfilled.

There is nothing in Nabokov's story to suggest that Lolita, like Humbert, is one of nature's freaks. She is presented rather as the norm of American youth which is given every opportunity of shedding its innocence without at the same time assuming the responsibilities that come with maturity. It is the warped youth of Lolita that is eventually the cause of her flat, uninteresting, frigid womanhood.

Except for Truman Capote, whose outlook is essentially humanitarian, and Kerouac, who seems satisfied with the "beat" escape from the status quo, the writers I have discussed, and many others as well, appear uncompromising in their indictment of the "new" woman. Their portrait of her emphasizes all the darker, negative qualities: loss of innocence, of selfhood, of sensibility; loss of the very capacity to love. On the other hand, not one of these writers is looking backward, sentimentally recalling models of another day. There are no contests between heroine and anti-heroine, such as Somerset Maugham, for instance, staged in *Of Human Bondage*. Rather, the writer appears to be facing up to reality and delving into its meaning.

And some are even searching for answers. Nabokov, whose criticism is sharpest, points an accusing finger at society. But more often the answer is sought in the less tangible area of human relationships. Modern woman is partially at least the work of modern man, reflecting his altered relationship to her. Men, it is suggested, have not fully accepted women as persons, have not achieved the total communicativeness which equality implies. Something more than sheer, undefined masculinity will be demanded of them as women abdicate the role of characterless abstractions of their sex. Not until men respond more wholeheartedly to that challenge (as Lawrence and Shaw have already demonstrated) will women be able to realize themselves fully as human beings, or at least as authentic women.

The case against the second sex in modern fiction is not as definitive as it may appear at the present moment. The fact that it is the object of a "case" at all—on a psychological, human level rather than on the merely social—may be a good omen. It may mean the beginning of the heroine's spiritual liberation, now long overdue.

1962

Crisis—in Fiction
or in Readership?

O ne of the paradoxes of the present cultural scene is the avidity with which we reach out to what is new in the arts at the same time that we confess our inability to enjoy what we have seized. We put pop art on our walls but call it "junk," we attend a concert by John Cage but snicker through the performance, and we buy the latest New Novel, only to leave it half-read. Does this mean that we are hypocrites, status-seekers in a culture-conscious era? One would think so if one were not also aware of an upsurge of responsiveness to artistic expression that seems to spring from a genuine need to identify with the creative impulses of the day.

What is lacking—if we must generalize—is not interest and desire but discrimination and taste. What makes the latter so difficult is the increasing diffusion of the arts and along with it the lifting of rigid barriers between the highbrow and the lowbrow, the esoteric and the commonplace. Thus on the one hand pop art can transform the beauty and power of expressionism into a simple dime-store commodity, and on the other an ingenious composer like Cage can manipulate the simplest patterns of sound into an elaborate system of silences. Both have elements that are easy to grasp, and both contain valid artistic impulses; but the vulgarization of the one and the over-refinement of the other preclude their giving the complete satisfaction of art.

In literature, an additional complication has come in the multiplicity of styles and the profusion of undigested critical opinion. The so-called crisis in fiction is perhaps in fact a crisis in *readership* of imaginative literature. The half-finished novel, the book of short stories barely begun and lying expectantly on the coffee table attest as much, if not more, to the reader's failure to understand as to the writer's failure to communicate. And if the reader is to be blamed, how much more so the critic who is so largely the promoter as well as the interpreter of contemporary writing?

It must be apparent to anyone who reads reviews of current fiction that the margin of error in making literary judgments has increased greatly. And for a very good reason. Too few critics (I am speaking now of critics writing for the daily press and weekly reviews) are looking closely enough at the novel and short story to see the changes that are taking place. Although discussions of modern fiction in the press have suddenly become popular, more confusion than ever seems to exist over what is good and what is bad, what is mere entertainment or mere polemic.

Taking part in a recent symposium on literary criticism, a noted critic confessed that criticism for him was "all a matter of individual opinion." Apologizing for the low level of criticism today, he bluntly concluded: "The decline of creation has led to the decline of criticism." And still more sourly, he added: "Nothing very much is happening in the novel."

With all due respect to this critic (who has since turned film reviewer), a great deal *is* happening in the novel—and this is partly the reason for the confusion. When something is only partly understood, when no attempt is made to understand it *on its own terms,* judgments are bound to become warped. Thus, books which deserve to be forgotten are overpraised, while those which merit attention are overlooked. It is not uncommon today to find the same book highly rated in one newspaper and utterly destroyed in another.

Perhaps this has always been a problem with criticism of contemporary writing. We are too close to it; we lack perspective. But a new element has been added to increase that difficulty. One of the striking aspects of contemporary American writing is its diversity. There is no predominant style, no predominant view. In this period of transition, as I see it, three distinctly different kinds of fiction—that is, serious fiction—are being written. (There may be more than three, but at least three are apparent, and they represent three distinct points of view.) The first two derive from earlier familiar conventions: the Realistic novel, as perfected by Balzac and Tolstoy, concerned with man in society, and viewed only objectively and pervasively; and Naturalistic fiction, centering on the nature of man, which in the hands of writers like Joyce and Virginia Woolf became, paradoxically, anti-realistic through its emphasis on inner states.

The third kind of fiction—the newest—combines these two styles, as it were, to achieve an effect that at its best is philosophic, and sometimes poetic. By probing at the same time the individual psyche and the material world in which it must operate, it seeks to mediate between the two—or at least to show that the need to mediate exists. I might add here that a major cause for the confusion in literary judgments these days—and our difficulty with a particular work—can be traced to the fact that too often one kind of novel is criticized or evaluated in terms of another. To be consistently competent, a critic today should be able to understand (if not equally appreciate) all three approaches. Certainly all three are valid.

But, while each is valid and intelligible on its own terms, the degree of success in each case will depend not only on whether the style the writer has chosen is consistently maintained, but also on whether it corresponds to the writer's personal faith, his basic vision.

Does the writer see man first and foremost as a social being, controlled by society's shifting standards? If he does, his best chances for success will be within the realistic tradition; bringing to it his knowledge of modern psychology, he will be able to write social criticism in the manner of a John O'Hara, a John Marquand, an Irwin Shaw or a Mary McCarthy (in her later works).

Or does the writer see man as alienated from the world at large, uneasy amidst its assumed realities, unwilling to conform to its ephemeral values? If he is this kind of writer, he should look for inspiration among the modernists, though his knowledge of how social pressures work on the individual will probably be larger and more subtle than that of a writer like D. H. Lawrence (who was to no small extent aware of the social dimension). Consequently, his characters, like those of a Carson McCullers, a James Purdy, or a Truman Capote, will often seem odd and abnormal, as neither Joyce's Molly Bloom nor Virginia Woolf's Mrs. Dalloway ever seemed. For the gap is growing ever wider between the sensitive, introspective individual and his mass-geared social environment.

Finally, does the writer see man as capable of transcending both his given nature and the values of his time and place? This last view—the most dynamic and positive one—must invariably absorb the two traditions mentioned. It is the view, I think, that much of the best of contemporary American fiction is striving to express.

I say *striving* because, except for the best of Hemingway and Faulkner (where this view partly found expression), and except for isolated works of present-day writers, a clear-cut tradition along this line has still to be established. Yet one can hardly avoid the impression that the most compelling writers in our midst are those who combine the realist's respect for tangible truths with the subjective writer's suspicion of fixed laws and generalities.

These new realists, or neo-realists, as we might call them, know that it is not possible to be truly alive and at the same time retreat from everyday reality—however much that may involve rituals and timetables for living. Far more conceivable in their view is the possibility that reality can be altered or redirected to serve their particular need or vision. Saul Bellow's recent statement that "vehement declarations of alienation are not going to produce great works of art" is indicative of the way the wind is blowing.

But how is the writer to engage reality? How is he to remain in it without conforming to it? More difficult, how can he hope to change it? By recognizing the distinction that exists between ourselves as functioning members of society (at the mercy of outside pressures) and as free spiritual entities, motivated solely from within. This is the task the writer sets himself: to confront and closely examine the self that is autonomous, unconditioned and instinctual—and having discovered it, to bring it forward, make it manifest.

For one example, let us look at the work of Eudora Welty. No one, I think, has been more successful than she in breaking down reality into its opposite components: the elusive and private, and the tangible and public. Anyone who has read her stories in *A Curtain of Green* or *The Golden Apples* knows how rich in local color and how precise in regional detail her writing is; anyone who knows her part of the South and fancies himself a student of human nature knows, too, how sharp her observations of character and manners can be. Yet it would be wrong to call her a social critic of the Realist school.

No matter how hard she may make you laugh at her characters or grow indignant at their fate, there is no acid in her laughter, no polemic in her compassion. No matter how directly her barbs may reflect on society-at-large, one knows that something else is more important. That something else has to do with her awareness of a destiny which human beings share in our time. Always her sympathy is fixed on the individual, that flawed being whose tragic—or often comic-seeming—plight is that he cannot achieve wholeness; who by his very quirks and unaccountable behavior betrays a fragmented, unintegrated self.

Sometimes, she will spotlight the gregarious character and show how he is a slave either to the family (that society within a society which is especially typical of the South) or to the false image of himself that society often creates. Other times, Miss Welty will fix her compassionate eye on the solitary and retiring character and show how by accommodating reality to the narrow limits of private experience he loses his chances for meaningful human contact and love—thus again frustrating his possibilities for wholeness. What is always implied in Eudora Welty's work, what prevents it from sounding bitter and negative, is the underlying conviction that it *is* possible, or should be possible, to break through the barriers of self and society.

Though totally different in other respects from Eudora Welty, Norman Mailer is another writer who is concerned with the interrelatedness of inner and outer reality. Though not in my opinion a major novelist, he is a striking example of a writer whom it is easy to overpraise (if one is impressed by his bold, sensational treatment of tabloid themes) or underpraise (if one misses the underlying Messianic fervor of his work). Where Miss Welty, like Chekhov, is *respectful* of tradition, if a little sad that it has worn thin, Mailer is *disrespectful*, as only a radical and anarchist can be.

By exposing the mythic nature of mass reality (the war and its delusions in *The Naked and the Dead;* Hollywood and its sham in *The Deer Park*), he means to explode the American Dream which has betrayed as much as it has been betrayed. What he wants is nothing less than a revolution—but a revolution *within* man. Thus he places his hope on the hipster—the self-exile of our time, the man who rejects order, permanence and continuity, whose secret of survival is what he calls "a new nervous system."

To satisfy the whims of the self—no matter where they may lead (in his novel *An American Dream*, they lead to nothing less than murder)—seems to Mailer preferable to submitting to the paralyzing untruths or myths of contemporary society. As he puts it in his famous essay, "The White Negro": "The only Hip morality . . . is to do what one feels whenever and wherever it is possible . . . to open the limits of the possible for oneself, for oneself alone, because that is one's need. Yet in widening the arena of the possible, one widens it reciprocally for others as well. . . ."

If Mailer fails to convince us—as André Gide, for instance, nearly convinces us—if too often his idealism misfires, it is because he asks us to accept too much on faith; he has not yet shown us that the hipster in the long run has a potential for goodness or even for happiness. Yet, he has unmistakenly and unequivocally faced a modern dilemma.

J. D. Salinger is a neo-realist in still another vein. You might call him a radical too, for he also expects a total transformation—a moral conversion that will heighten our capacity to perceive truth and diminish the corrupting power over us of a mass-directed society. Because *The Catcher in the Rye* was steeped in all that is characteristic of urban American life, he was invariably praised as a novelist of manners. But like Eudora Welty's, his real concern is elsewhere. In more recent works, *Seymour: An Introduction* and *Franny and Zooey,* he has emerged as a transcendental writer, one might say even a religious one.

The phoniness, vulgarity and cruel indifference of the world are exposed only to show how they are countered by innocence, purity and a spontaneous, gratuitous love. His characters, far from underprivileged, and misfits only in the sense that they are intellectually superior to their environment (Seymour and his brothers have been quiz kids), are riddled with anxiety, pulled now in one direction, now in another. In the two novels of the Glass family, Salinger shows his characters' progress from search for self to search for salvation and finally reconciliation. Wisdom for his saint-heroes comes to mean rising above their injured sensibilities, their closely guarded egos, to recognize their common bond with others.

One could give other instances of writers arguing for reconciliation through conversion. There is the impassioned voice of James Baldwin, rebellious only because he seeks acceptance of a reality which black and white share: their human nature. A gentler voice is that of Bernard Malamud, staunch in his compassion for hero-victims who are morally superior to their oppressors, whose triumphs often lie in failure. There is Saul Bellow, whose works of high comedy and irony *(The Adventures of Augie March, Henderson the Rain King,* and *Herzog)* deal with adventurer-individualists who discover that real freedom lies in commitment. There is Ralph Ellison, whose Invisible

Man, reborn, affirms: "The hibernation is over. . . . I must shake off the old skin and come up for breath. . . . My world has become one of infinite possibilities."

Conventional realism with its deterministic faith has given way to a transcendent realism that says man can, if he will, reverse the course of his destiny and mediate between the needs of the private self and those of the world—which it is his *privilege* to shape.

What this group of writers seems most intent on conveying is that modern man can resist the deadening impact of a mechanized world through an enlarged awareness of his human capacity. But this is only partly *existential* faith, the wind that has blown our way from a desperate, war-ravaged France. Unlike his European counterpart, the American existential writer appears to resist the knowledge that man's fate is an absurdity. Perhaps because finality is not congenial to the American temperament. Or because his faith remains unshaken in the unalterable truths—love, freedom, goodness—with their promise of redemption. There is a characteristic quote in a novel by Herbert Gold called *The Optimist:* "How does a person discover which of his thousand possibilities is his real self? He wanted to discover the meaning of his reactions in the world and to give himself an idea of himself."

It is this optimistic belief in "a thousand possibilities of the self," this kind of relentless search into "the meaning of reactions that give the self an idea of the self" that has complicated the modern American novel. But it has made it new. And it has made it worthy again of our closest attention.

1965

The Flight from Innocence:* England's Newest Literary Generation

There is a poignant moment at the end of John Osborne's play *Look Back in Anger* when the unhappy heroine, Alison, stripped of all her defenses, cries out:

> I don't want to be neutral. I don't want to be a saint. I want to be a lost cause. I want to be corrupt and futile.

At that instant, it is as if Alison, like Ibsen's famous Nora, were transformed from a mere character in a play into a social reality, voicing a point of view that in her case is symptomatic of an emerging generation in England. Alison's revolt, if such it may be called, is directed inward. Like Nora, she has given up miracles in favor of life. But it is not on her doll's house that she expects to shut the door; it is on her old self—on her romantic faith in her innocence.

*From "The Flight from Innocence: England's Newest Literary Generation," by Nona Balakian, *Books Abroad,* Vol. 33, #3. Copyright 1959 by the University of Oklahoma Press.

In his ability to distill the philosophical essence of his time and to create authentic character—character that is so contemporary that it is still unacknowledged—Osborne is not unique in the England of the fifties, though as a tragedian he is perhaps the most provocative of the so-called Angry Young Men. Along with him there emerged in quick succession a group of writers, all under forty, whose insight into the contemporary scene is the most striking thing about their work. The most interesting among them are the novelists: Kingsley Amis, John Wain, Iris Murdoch, John Braine, and J. P. Donleavy—all writing in a comic genre but essentially not less serious than Osborne. If any misapprehension exists on this score, it is largely, one suspects, because they have so slyly hidden the object of their "revolt" ("flight" would be more accurate) behind a candid façade of self-deflation and/or self-mockery.

Because they have been taken at face value, as "comic" or "protest" writers, they have been found wanting by the elder critics of England who have compared them to their classic predecessors in these genres. In America, further confusion has been created by the absence of familiarity with the present-day English social scene. As a result, critics have turned from evaluation of their works to the personalities of the writers or, at best, to a superficial consideration of the novelist's or playwright's protagonists. Amidst all the shouting, little thought has been given to their place in the stream of the English novel or drama and their departure from certain established literary traditions.

As if to confound the critics further, these writers have resisted being identified with each other. Being English, they have a native distaste for literary "movements": they cherish their originality too much. Beyond that, they have been repelled by the term that has been used to describe them. To call them "angry," they feel, is to simplify their aim, and worse still to distort it by suggesting the aggressive "protest" of the proletarian novel or play.

Anger, the blatant anger of social protest, can only generate more anger of that sort: it cannot induce critical thought or hope to overhaul established concepts. These sophisticated writers find it much more effective to turn to comedy—or, in its absence, to macabre irony and a touching play of contrasts. What they have in common beyond their responses to the same problems is an impious and unromantic view in which anger figures as a detergent, clearing the air for a new look at reality. In this respect, they are more nearly the heirs of G. B. Shaw than of Orwell, of Brecht and Anouilh than of O'Casey.

Though they are quite indifferent to Shaw's social dictum, the novelists especially have assimilated the two essential methods of the master: his shock tactics and his habit of paradox. The difference here is that the shock is aimed at a much lower level: in the commonness of speech, in outlandish behavior and in zany, ribald humor. Nor is their idea of paradox simply to play the devil's advocate; juxtaposing the absurd and the accepted, they aim to undermine the premise of faith itself.

Their most striking paradox is perhaps their hero, a combination of rogue and uneasy solid citizen. Located in the lower rungs of the social structure, these heroes are neither sentimentalized in the manner of Dickens nor regarded with indulgence as eccentrics. Cowardly and suspicious in their human relations, motivated solely by self-interest, uninhibited in language and disrespectful of women, they are heroic only in their resistance to the straitjacket mold tendered to them by society. Self-confessed failures, their only saving grace is a heightened awareness and startling lack of self-delusion. Indeed, they are rogues not for the mere pleasure of it, but of necessity, being in flight from the accepted norm.

Trapped in socially embarrassing situations and in the mad traffic of life, they promote, at least for a while, an atmosphere that is hectic and charged with surprise. But the hearty laughter usually does not last. Monotony sets in, and gradually, as the story's paradoxical meaning is revealed, we begin to feel uncomfortable. We are suddenly not remote enough to indulge in the savage laughter of Evelyn Waugh, nor yet close enough to enjoy the tolerant one of Joyce Cary. The sardonic laughter of Shaw fits best.

It is, in fact, in the quality of their humor that these writers betray their moral fervor. Writing from within a newly emerging intellectual middle class, they are as far removed from the Bloomsbury tradition of sensibility and psychological refinement as from the novel of social protest. Where new problems have been created, the old values will not do. In the paternalistic welfare state, little relevance remains to Shaw's early-century socialistic notion that "the worst of our crimes is poverty . . . . money destroys base people." Poverty is no longer the big bogey, nor is money the equivalent of culture. ("Money and culture, money and charm, who can separate them?" railed Orwell's hero in another age.) It is not *insecurity* these writers fear but a certain kind of material *security* which promotes a cozy apathy and dehumanization. ("How I long for a little human enthusiasm," Osborne's Jimmy Porter cries out. "I want to hear a warm thrilling voice cry out Hallelujah! I'm alive!") Conformity and standardization are seen as dangerous threats to the individualism once cherished by all classes.

Between the comfort-seeking masses and the new intellectual the breach is expanding. Through government scholarships and individual effort, these bright young people have lifted themselves mentally and spiritually out of their working-class backgrounds. Traditional social barriers, however, still make their position among the privileged classes practically untenable. Hence their dilemma. Identified with neither end of the social structure, the new intellectuals are left with standards that lack meaning. To turn inward, to feed on their own resources, becomes the only possible solution.

Henceforth, only their own intelligence can fortify them against the pressures of mass culture, the tricks of "the hidden persuaders." To protect their sense of truth, of integrity and justice, they become skeptical and even cynical. As products of socialism, they are disillusioned about the power of social reform to solve human problems and contribute a sense of purpose to life. But if this completes the pattern of negativism, it does not shut out the possibility of a new faith—as a closer examination of their work reveals.

It might be illuminating to consider, first, three nonfiction works from this group of writers which have been indiscriminately quoted in support of arbitrary views about their aims. There is, first of all, Kingsley Amis's essay "Socialism and the Intellectual," which has been mistaken for an explicit avowal of these young writers' noncommitment not only to politics but to life itself. Amis, an academic as well as a poet and novelist, actually directs his skepticism specifically at politics. Moreover, his criticism has an authentic basis. Having been himself a former dabbler in socialist politics, he holds to sharp account the politically oriented writers of a previous generation— Auden, C. Day Lewis, Orwell—whom he suspects (offering proof) of turning to politics from "a kind of self-administered therapy for personal difficulties rather than for the reform of society." For himself, he refuses to become involved in cases which have only an abstract meaning for him.

The basic attitude of intellectual honesty, reflected in Amis's ineptly written article, is echoed—with variations—in the work of Colin Wilson and Stuart Holroyd. Handicapped by their youth, and in Wilson's case by the initial adulation of overeager critics, neither writer has been given a fair hearing. It is easy to dismiss Wilson's *The Outsider* (1956) as a hopelessly pretentious and overrated work. But because it is ostensibly an honest and earnest effort by a member of the new intellectual class, it has a certain extrinsic value as an index to contemporary thought in England.

Reading modern literature from Dostoevsky to Camus, Wilson has inevitably stumbled on the lonely figure of alienated modern man: "the outsider," as he calls him. Unwilling to live in "the comfortable, insulated world of the bourgeois, accepting what he sees and touches as reality," the existentialist outsider "asserts his sense of anarchy," not simply from "the need to cock a snook at respectability," but from "a distressing sense that *the truth must be told at all cost*." What

Wilson proposes as a corollary to the English brand of existentialism is the hope of a spiritually higher type of man (a kind of embodiment of Shaw's Life Force) who has moved from superstition to disbelief but who must come finally to a new vision, based on metaphysical awareness.

Using much the same phrases, Stuart Holroyd in *Emergence from Chaos* (1957) makes a similar plea for what he calls "the religious attitude," which he defines as faith in man's ability to change. "Freedom is an inner condition," he echoes Wilson:

> The free man is he who has a firm grasp on himself . . . . he is an externally existing individual who stands absolutely responsible for his actions before God.

Both Wilson and Holroyd insist that their concern is for the improvement of *men* themselves and not merely their social environment. Their passionate desire to widen the areas of consciousness exonerates them from the charge of escapism. By relating philosophy to artistic effort they have set the groundwork for visions of a new reality, a new faith.

Midway between the political negativism of Amis and the philosophical affirmation of Wilson and Holroyd is the position of the man of feeling, the artist. Within England's new literary generation, no one perhaps more aptly represents him than John Osborne.

It is the absence of "the religious attitude" that unconsciously gnaws at the heart of Osborne's heroes, especially of Jimmy Porter—who, coincidentally, made his debut at the Royal Court Theatre in London the same year that *The Outsider* was published. Jimmy Porter, the semi-educated, seedy, desperate young man whose longing for refinement has trapped him into marrying a woman socially his superior, is too vulgar, disagreeable and uncouth to suggest a tragic hero. But his predicament—the individual's isolation in his environment—has genuinely tragic dimensions. What on the surface seem purposeless anger and snarling cynicism have their root in an acute disenchantment that has not yet found release in quiescence.

Jimmy, who is content to run a sweets stall, is not concerned about lack of money (though there is a short supply of it in the one-room flat that is his home in the Midlands). The cause of his frustration is not that obvious; what rankles in him is the realization that he does not "belong." Nobody hears his words when he speaks, much less understands his heart when it aches. What he has imagined as philosophical serenity in his wife, Alison, has been revealed as placid acceptance, an attitude he comes to connect with the false timidity of the "genteel," and which he sees as "escape from the pain of being alive. And most of all from love." His feeling for her is further complicated by a repressed sense of guilt toward friends of former days whom he has abandoned in the course of improving himself intellectually.

These are the conditions he cannot escape. But they do not wholly bind him; in brief moments when he is moved by enthusiasm, curiosity, pity, and the desire for pure thought, he suggests the potential of a superior human being desperately seeking fulfillment.

It is in the bitterly ironic ending of the play that Osborne's ambiguous feeling about Jimmy is finally resolved. Suddenly acquiescent before Alison's outburst (quoted above), he leads her back with him to the make-believe world of "very timid little animals" which had been their shield against reality. Essentially unequipped to face depths, he thus reverts to romantic escapism.

This mixture of pathos and irony makes even stronger fare in Osborne's next play, *The Entertainer*, which was written and produced the following year, in 1957. A *danse macabre* in the Brecht manner, it demonstrates even more strikingly the futility of protest. Archie Rice (so superbly played by Sir Laurence Olivier), a loud-mouthed, third-rate vaudeville comedian, so common and conformist on the surface, is sufficiently educated and aware to know the small scale of his own tragedy and to know also that there is nothing anybody can do about it. This is how he explains why "every night is party night," and why it is wise to "whoop it up" while you can, before your son gets killed in some remote war in the Suez:

> Do you know why? Because we're dead beat and down and outs. . . . Why, we've problems that nobody's heard of, we're characters out of something nobody believes in. . . . We don't even succeed in anything. We're a nuisance. . . .

Older and wiser than Jimmy, Archie can repress his anger, but his self-mockery cuts to the core.

In the same defeatist spirit, George Dillon in *Epitaph for George Dillon* (Osborne's first play written with Anthony Creighton) anticipates the death of his dream of being a great playwright. Adept at deceiving others, he will not deceive himself; before the last act, he knows that he can only succeed through compromise. The only audience he can write for are the insensitive millions whose "existence is one great cliché that they carry about with them like a snail in its little house."

Osborne is pitiless toward his "outsiders": for a while their anger spurts and engulfs in vituperation those who stand in the path of their self-fulfillment. Then, in a moment of truth, their anger fizzes out in the knowledge that transcendence for them is impossible.

Kingsley Amis's novel *Lucky Jim,* which preceded *Look Back in Anger* by two years, has on the face of it little in common with the somber plays of John Osborne. Its bantering *commedia dell'arte* manner and happy-go-lucky hero, it would appear, are calculated to do nothing more than entertain. Jim Dixon, the cocky, baby-faced university don on-the-make, would probably not have the vaguest notion what Osborne's characters were raving about. Their speeches indeed would bore him. In his kind of world, action, not words, is what counts; having "scholarshipped" himself out of his working-class background, and by the skin of his teeth become a junior lecturer in a provincial university, Jim has made it his life's mission to maintain the *status quo.* Considering his lack of integral relation to the academic life, this is no small matter.

Jim, whose "policy is to read as little as possible of any given book," is contemptuous not only of learning but of the people who pursue it. What he most distrusts about the academic world is the presence in it of old bores like Ned Welch, his pompous, incompetent department head. To ingratiate himself with Welch, Jim must also put up with Welch's son, Bertrand, whose snobbish attitudes grate on Jim's innate hostility toward the upper classes.

Yet Jim would be the last to minimize the advantages of his position. Unlike Jimmy Porter, who is an "outsider" *manqué,* Jim Dixon is ready to join the "insiders" and play the racket—at least to all intents and purposes. In his private underground, he gets back at them: he purges himself of his hostile feelings by making facial expressions do the work of angry words. Beyond that, his hidden contempt expresses itself in an impulsive, loutish behavior: he hijacks taxis, makes fake phone calls, and on a weekend at the Welches' gets drunk and accidentally burns the bedclothes; the following morning, he shocks a fellow guest by swallowing a fried egg whole. By juxtaposing every foolish action of Jim's against the phony attitudes and manners of those whom he must outwit to survive, Amis creates, with his rich comic gifts, a topsy-turvy Alice-in-Wonderland atmosphere in which values are hopelessly dislocated. Yet couched in the comedy is a harsh truth: in his search for status, Jim has had to compromise his better self. "It was luck you needed all along," he comments smugly at the end, accepting his good fortune as he escapes into success outside the ivied walls.

As a product of changing England, Jim is an original. Yet the novel is played out mainly in classic style, a feeling for the human comedy superseding an eye for social anomaly. This is less true of Amis's next novel, *That Uncertain Feeling* (1955), in which characters and situations are particularized to make a more striking novel of social comment. No quick summary can convey the rich comedy which results when a mildly ambitious, class-conscious young librarian, John Lewis, falls into the clutches of an influential *femme fatale*. But mention should be made of what is perhaps the classic example in this literature of the use of slapstick humor to parody romantic love. Nearly caught in the midst of a "torrid" love scene in the home of his paramour, John, in perfect control, assumes the disguise of a plumber and engages the lady's husband in conversation. Lacking Jim's good luck and his glib social sense, John is caught between loyalty to himself as a reluctant Don Juan, and to his wife, who represents respectability. In the end, he retreats into the blessings of security, which are as tight as a noose around his neck.

John Wain, who has often been compared to Kingsley Amis, is actually less of a spontaneous humorist and a more consciously intellectual writer. Born in 1925, he is three years Amis's junior, has a similar Oxford and middle-class background, and is, like him, also a poet—one of the so-called University Wits. Wain has disclaimed that he is a spokesman for his generation, his nation, or his class, and reading his work (four novels so far) alongside of Amis's, one can see why. The dilemmas of his characters do not specifically derive from the contemporary social scene but rather from a kind of philosophical consciousness, an erring concept of freedom.

Charles Lumley, the derelict hero in *Hurry on Down* (published in America as *Born in Captivity*), just down from the university, stumbles into one meaningless job after another in an unsuccessful attempt to locate his social roots. If he is too self-centered to care about the working class (from which he is a refugee), he also lacks Jim Dixon's unwilling fascination with the privileged classes. But most of all it is the middle class he distrusts, fearing its power to absorb him with its lures of comfort and security. Hugging his individualism, he determines to remain outside the class structure, preferring self-imposed exile to "the suffocating sense of utter inability to communicate" which he feels even in the presence of his girl. Lumley, like "the outsider," allegedly sees "too deep and too much," but he does not see deep enough: he scarcely knows *himself*. It is not until much later that he becomes aware of his real motive for rejecting society: flight from commitment to life, which stems from an absence of moral and spiritual fiber. "Neutrality" was what he wanted; but, as he puts it, "the running fight between himself and society had ended in a draw."

In Wain's *The Contenders* (1958), the protagonist is a "neutralist" with a difference: one who has no regrets. A provincial newspaper reporter (appropriately the novel's narrator), Joe Shaw is only loosely "committed" to his local community and in a lackadaisical way to his two chums from school days, whose rise to fame and fortune he relates. Lazy, unambitious, indifferent to social status, and wary of women, he has two qualities which enable him to keep an ironic distance from life: a wisecracking sense of humor and a cynical acceptance of every man's self-sufficiency. Telling the story as it happens, he is content during most of the novel to sit on the fence while his two friends knock each other about in the race for success, social prominence, and the women who make these worthwhile. "I could sit about and see the funny side of other people's emotional problems," he says, "because I hadn't got any myself." Like Lumley, he would rather be free than successful.

Only, Joe Shaw is not really free. In the end, like Porter, he is trapped by love into commitment. Unexpectedly falling in love with his artist friend's latest prize, Shaw suddenly develops an aggressive energy that marks him as a potential contender. It is a sardonic conclusion to a novel that on the surface is full of satiric fun and surprises. Deliberately colloquial, with aimless, idiomatic dialogue that speaks not only for the locale but for the professions it is depicting, it has an almost *American* flavor.

A study in success which bears comparison with *The Contenders* is John Braine's *Room at the Top* (1957). A librarian by vocation, born in Yorkshire in the same year as Amis, Braine writes with a curious combination of naïveté and hard-headed realism, a slick magazine facileness and bright originality of phrasing. Though in many respects a true representative of this group of novels, *Room at the Top* is in one respect old-fashioned. For this story of the go-getting Joe Lampton, who unconsciously sets out to conquer the world, who loses his soul and is duly repentant, is an explicitly moralizing one.

Joe Lampton, the story's narrator, is much more cunning than Wain's Joe Shaw: a modern Julien Sorel, committed to no accepted morality or convention, he is a man completely true to himself (as far as he understands himself), yet true to no one else. Midway through the story of his climb from rags to riches, as he rationalizes the betrayal of his girl, he admits:

What has happened to me is exactly what I willed to happen. I am my own draughtsman. Destiny, force of events, good or bad fortune—all that battered repertory company can be thrown right out of my story.

Joe's wants—what indeed he considers his rights—are clear-cut: "An Aston-Martin, a three-guinea linen shirt and a girl with a Riviera suntan." Fired by the romance of money, which he also sees as the elixir of sex, Joe is at all times aware of what he is about:

There is a transparent barrier between myself and strong emotion. I feel what is correct for me to feel; I go through the necessary motions. But I cannot delude myself that I care. . . .

It is only when he realizes that he has been responsible for the death of the woman he loved that the real burden of his degradation is brought home to him. When told that nobody blames him for what happened, he replies: "Oh my God, that's the trouble." The moral conscience which Joe imagined he could suppress asserts itself when life forces him to become involved.

Despite the pathos of its ending, the prevailing mood of *Room at the Top* is one of good-humored satire. For this reason, though Braine can write violent sexy scenes with evident relish, there is never a suggestion of lewdness.

This cannot so truthfully be said of J. P. Donleavy's *The Ginger Man* (1957). A Brooklyn-born ex-G.I., Donleavy does not technically belong in this group, but by reason of long residence in Britain and of his characteristic response to its social scene, he has understandably become identified with Amis, Wain, and Co.

Though not so cunning as Joe Lampton, Sebastian Dangerfield, "the ginger man," is even more of a cad. A drunken, destructive lecher who revels in vulgar language and outrageous behavior, he has none of Joe's excuses. He has never really been penniless; indeed when we meet him he is sitting in the lap of privilege as a former G.I. studying law on the Bill of Rights. True, enforced residence in Dublin with a wife and small child in cramped and antiquated quarters is not exactly conducive to intellectual effort—but then, for Dangerfield, a much lesser excuse would also do. Writing of him sometimes in the first person, sometimes in the third, Donleavy seems purposely to confuse his portrait, as if to undermine the reader's certainty.

A characteristic of these novels and plays which I have not so far stressed is a consistent irreverence toward a subject which has been nearly sacrosanct in British and American literature: namely, women as objects of romantic love. From Lucky Jim's and Joe Shaw's cautious, distrustful attitude toward women to Jimmy Porter's vituperation of Alison, to Joe Lampton's violent sexuality, we can see various degrees of resentment toward what they regard distinctly as the *weaker* sex. The women in these novels and plays are generally unreliable, insincere, easily given to compromise; in their need of security, they represent a threat to man's urge for freedom and self-identity. We have seen Amis's gently mocking treatment of passion; in *The Ginger Man,* sex itself becomes the target of ridicule that verges on the offensive.

The indignities which Dangerfield makes his wife, Marion, suffer are characteristic of his sadistic spirit of fun. Married like Porter above his social station, he has no real point of contact with his wife outside the physical one; indeed his relationship with her, even after some years of married life, is essentially no different from his relationship with the women he chooses at random to make love to. As a result, his cynicism toward sex, like his cynicism toward religion, is tinged with a dark humor.

In Dangerfield's world utter chaos prevails. But unlike the true "outsider," he cannot face the void. He prefers to escape into the pleasures of the flesh, into a wild humor that anaesthetizes anger, and into unregenerate delinquency. His only virtue, in this case a dubious one, is that he will not conform. "This is the main thing," he brags at the end; "I've kept the dignity."

With the possible exception of John Wain, who is a philosophically oriented writer, and John Osborne, who has the artist's intuitive capacity to pinpoint the nature of a wound, none of the writers so far discussed has shown himself concerned with specific solutions. The group, however, has its philosopher, or at least a writer with a distinct philosophy. Publishing her first novel, *Under the Net* (1954), at the slightly more advanced age of thirty-five, Iris Murdoch is generally recognized as the most distinguished prose writer in the group. She is also the most experimental and inventive, combining a genuine comic gift with a deep compassion.

It is significant that Miss Murdoch, a lecturer on philosophy at Oxford, began her career with a critical study of the existentialist writer Jean-Paul Sartre. One no sooner makes this statement than one wants to retract it. For her brand of existentialism has not the slightest ring of Sartre's gloominess or of Camus's solemnity. In a curiously oblique way she adjusts this abstract philosophy to her own aims, which involve, among other things, a search for the meaning of love and its frequent elusiveness.

Essentially an artist, Iris Murdoch expresses her ideas as much through form as through content. What is difficult for the unsuspecting reader is not only the obliqueness of her style but the variableness of her mood, which swings like a pendulum from comic to pathetic, satiric to near tragic. All manner of crazy, impossible things happen in her novels—the abduction of a caged dog; a girl swinging on a chandelier; a woman surrendering alternately to brothers who agree to share her; a man taking cold-cure inoculations to find shelter—things that outrage not only our sense of propriety or decency but our very knowledge of what is *possible.* Iris Murdoch seems not afraid to create *unreality,* or *super*-reality, if it will show us life afresh, free of the platitudes which cling to the familiar and commonplace.

Most of the time her characters, like Samuel Beckett's, seem to be waiting for something—perhaps for the spark that will ignite them to life; paralyzed by self-consciousness and unable to communicate with other human beings, they drift into fantastic adventures.

Jack Donoghue, the marginal man in *Under the Net,* has a superficial resemblance to Orwell's literary hack, Gordon Comstock, in *Keep the Aspidistra Flying!* But while Orwell's hero counts himself a victim of society, Jack blames no one but himself:

> I am talented but lazy . . . it is not in myself to make myself responsible to other people. I find it hard enough to pick my way along.

The independence he cherishes is immune to poverty or insecurity, but it is made hollow by the absence of something more intangible, the companionship of another human being. Because an inverted romanticism has made it impossible for him to achieve intimacy, he has never come near to understanding Anna, the woman he imagined that he loved:

> When does one ever know a human being? Perhaps only after one realizes the impossibility of knowledge and renounces the desire for it. But then what one achieves is no longer knowledge, it is simply a kind of co-existence; and this, too, is one of the guises of love.

The philosophical message of *The Bell* (1958), though stated explicitly in certain passages, is also inherent in the pattern of her story. The setting is Imber Court, a High Anglican utopia where a varied and ill-assorted lay community is trying to emulate the example of the nuns in a nearby Benedictine convent. The action revolves around the community's bestowal of a new bell upon the Abbey to replace the one that had mysteriously disappeared many centuries earlier. It is typical of Murdoch's teasing manner that the allegorical and symbolic trappings of the tale offer no real clue to her philosophical meaning. In a general sense, the convent represents the authority of the Church, while its spokesman, the Abbess, represents the wisdom of the true devotee whose faith is not distinct from human compassion. The two stand in sharp contrast to Imber Court, which, as the Abbess puts it, has been created "for those who could live neither in the world nor out of it."

It is a measure of Miss Murdoch's versatility that she can be equally sympathetic with characters on both ends of the human spectrum. On the one end is the young wife Dora—a social misfit with a gift for upsetting applecarts. A kind of feminine version of Lucky Jim, she is the perfect foil for the pretentiousness and conceit of men like her husband and the religious zealot James Pace. Conceived in comedy, Dora is not wholly an object of ridicule—her little weaknesses, her spontaneity are much too charming. In the same way, though conceived in tragedy, Michael Meade, the high-minded homosexual, is not a pitiful figure. More than the sum of his problems, he is a man seeking self-esteem and an outlet for his enormous will to goodness. It is in his mouth that Iris Murdoch puts her message:

> To live in innocence . . . we need all the strength that we can muster—and to use our strength we must know where it lies. This is the struggle, pleasing surely in the sight of God, to become more fully and deeply the person that we are.

But Michael's warning that spiritual salvation lies in a deeper understanding of our limitations and individual needs comes too late. As it becomes evident that individual problems do not respond to pure theory and authority, the community is dissolved.

In my concern to uphold these writers against the charges of triviality and escapism, I have not been able to do more than suggest their purely literary achievements. Turning to these briefly now, I think it is only fair to admit that, on the whole, these representatives of England's newest literary generation do not yet speak with the authority of great art. Often they give the impression of awkwardness in dealing with philosophical ideas borrowed from the continent and technical innovations appropriated from America. In the matter of form, they are not unadventurous, but they have still to explore the full possibilities of the post-psychological novel in which analysis of motive is wholly implicit. Thoughtful, often original, in their approach to character, they bring a subtle knowledge of the pliability of human nature, but their obsession with certain patterns of behavior tends to make their characters, after a while, too predictable and hence uninteresting. Finally, they have still to meet the challenge of all creative work which derives its impact from specific reference to the contemporary scene. Too often because they assume knowledge on our part which we may not have, we miss the urgency of the situations that are played out.

Yet these failings apart, we cannot ignore the impression they convey of intellectual alertness and a vital sensitivity. These writers are bringing to the English novel and drama new ideas, a new style, and a new sense of the tragicomic essence of life. It is significant, too, I think, that the generation of the fifties is no longer feeding on the achievement of the twenties. If they cannot yet clearly see what lies ahead, they can at least say with G. B. Shaw: "It is enough that there is a beyond."

1959

The New Transcendentalists: A Quasi-Religious Mode in American Fiction

A sea-change has come over the anti-hero of American fiction, and if we are reading the signs right, his conversion is transforming modern literature. That arrogant, irresolute picaresque who became the trademark of an era has acquired a new dimension that threatens to upset the applecart and make him humanly—if not socially—respectable. Under his hard, protective shell, there is the glimmer of a "soul"—achieved at no small cost to easy disbelief. Alternating between flight and commitment, he has curbed his ego and discovered the Family of Man—in whose behalf he vehemently affirms. In a spiritually abused world, he has instinctively moved toward transcendence—and become "the new religious." Witness the following examples:

Harry Angstrom, the "absurd" hero of John Updike's *Rabbit, Run* (1960), is an habitual runner from spiritually abused worlds who suffers from religious anguish: "If God doesn't exist," he asks, "why does anything?"

Saul Bellow's perennially self-deceived middle-aged professor "Herzog" (1964), who contains his aggressions by writing letters he never mails, thus states his relationship to God: "I have desired your unknowable will, taking it and you, without symbols. Everything of intensest significance. Especially if divested of me."

Zooey in *Franny and Zooey* (1961), one of J. D. Salinger's family of "seers"—the Glasses—persuades his sister that life is worth living by "introducing" her to Christ, "the most intelligent man in the Bible . . . who knew that we're carrying the Kingdom of Heaven within us."

The unjustly persecuted Russian-Jew in Malamud's *The Fixer* conquers with a spiritual strength that owes nothing to the God of the *shtetl,* who "goes around with the Law in both hands."

It is not my intent on the basis of the above to claim a religious revival in American fiction. These capsule reports and quotes could easily be countered by as many others revealing an opposite point of view. What I venture to suggest is that at a time when "The Death of God" is receiving so much publicity, the search for God has become a dominant, urgent and authentic preoccupation of quite a number of current novelists. No one familiar with the works of these writers needs to be told that there is no doctrinal connotation in this writing such as one finds in the works of Mauriac, Bernanos, Graham Greene and Flannery O'Connor. Where always in the religious novel there is a logical course of cause and effect that operates even when the surface impression is "absurd," an inevitable sequence of sin, guilt, damnation, retribution, salvation that assures us its message will not be lost, in these quasi-religious novels, on the other hand, not only is the vocabulary changed but no familiar sequence is visible. Though God is named and salvation implied, neither has the usual connotation. The key words have become "quest," "unity," "possibility" and "transcendence."

Though John Updike's "Rabbit" Angstrom shuns responsibility, he faces not retribution but a new-found integrity. And Malamud's "Fixer" must die though he has been victimized. There is obviously no clear-cut moral to be drawn, and the religious element is reduced to that of an "experience"—an illumination or epiphany—to be shared.

Confusion is compounded by the fact that the illumination is reached in the very midst of mundane concerns and physical aspects of life. It is easy to miss the religious overtones in books where the religious motif is introduced obliquely, as it were, through the side door. Sometimes it remains quite hidden (as in the work of Katherine Anne Porter and Flannery O'Connor); while at other times, as in Mailer's *An American Dream,* it is deliberately subverted. (But of these last two types of "religious works" another essay must be written.) Not to be denied, moreover, is the fact that in many instances the religious stance or attitude is essentially pallid or so poorly integrated into the warp and woof of the novel that it will understandably and deservedly be missed.

However indirect or oblique the approach, religious themes have had a strong enough pull on American fiction to bring about a drastic departure from negativism, or "the destructive element," as Stephen Spender called the prevailing mode of modern literature. The change became accelerated and pronounced because a closer relationship has been established between the author and his characters than has been possible in modern literature for a long time. Though the anti-hero was initially launched as a realistic creation, a symptomatic phenomenon with an autonomous life of his own (Donleavy's *The Ginger Man* of 1958 is an example), he gradually drew closer and closer to the author's thought, until today it can be said that—except in rare instances—he shares in the novelist's vision, his understanding, his purpose. Even that quasi-ironist, Saul Bellow, is, in the final analysis, behind the general positive stance of his hero. Say Herzog and Bellow: ". . . if the unexplained life is not worth living, the explained life is unbearable, too. 'Synthesize or perish!' Is that the new law?"

But whether or not the pendulum has swung, one thing is clear: it is no longer necessary to be lost, disenchanted, alienated to become a significant writer in America. This is not to say that the reversal is complete. The final curtain has not yet rung on the modernist movement, and in the wings, those flawed humanists, the dark humorists (Barth, Burroughs, Heller and Pynchon), are still inwardly repeating the prayer in the Hemingway story, "Our Nada Who Art in Nada," as they escape with laughter from the void.

Though in France writers in this vein are called "the new wave," in America, where dark humor has never languished (if sustained only in our comics), they do not seem so avant-garde. With all the impression they leave of anarchy and amorality, the works of this extremist group of writers seem actually to present less of a threat to the existing orthodoxies—whether literary, political or social—than the works of novelists we call "the new religious." And with reason. The negative element of the modernists, for instance, has become so entrenched in the critical values of the day that a Saul Bellow can shock the academics—as he recently did at the P.E.N. Congress—by attacking "the deadening orthodoxy of academicians" who find it enlightening to "expose, disenchant, hate and experience disgust."

In the same way, political extremism has painted such a dark picture of race relations that a Ralph Ellison will seem to be taking a meliorist view when he objects—as Ellison did at a Senate Subcommittee hearing—that Harlem is not a place of decay but a place of "historical and social memory" which must be changed but not destroyed. As for the social scene, only the inescapable fact of the great apathy and loss of a sense of commitment could have made possible the acceptance of that unhealthy, confused but very vital affirmation of the Beats. Because the movement degenerated, however, into a fad that had less to do with belief than with personal habits (clothes, morals, etc.), the ideological content of their works has become suspect on all sides. Only their aesthetics as poets seems at the moment to have some interest.

But if this self-conscious insistence on affirmation were only a matter of shock value, it would be of no more than passing interest. That it is more than that—that it reflects an authentic mood of the period, or at least one that is in the making—can be established when we view it from the perspective provided by literary history. Until the modernists came, American literature always seesawed between two extremes of yea-saying and nay-saying, with no particular reference to the social scene. Long before the modernist movement had reached these shores, American writers had known the mood of dissidence and alienation—what Melville had called "the power of darkness." Melville himself, as well as Hawthorne, Poe, and in a milder way James, had questioned the capacity of man to see reality and measure the truth; without being "religious" writers as such, they had affirmed the presence of evil in the heart of man. But at the same time, an upsurge of faith in man, in his possibilities in a democratic society, had emerged in the middle of the last century under the impetus of the Transcendentalists—Emerson, Thoreau, Theodore Parker and many others were the movers behind this faith.

But with the coming of World War I, and in fact in a period before that, various factors converged to make the negative view predominate for a long stretch in American literature. There was first the influence of the literary modernists in Europe—Joyce, Eliot, Pound and others. There was the fact of expatriation, which gave Americans a sense of alienation from home ground. There was, later, the war, and still later the Depression—all elements which made it impossible to be anything but somber and deeply skeptical about the human potential. Nor did the desperate humanism of a Hemingway and a Faulkner, the utopianism of a Saroyan and a Steinbeck, the cosmic view of a Thornton Wilder suggest the possibilities for a religious revival.

But by the middle of this century, the mood began to change. In 1950 the *Partisan Review* was conducting a symposium of prominent intellectuals to determine what was behind "the present revival of religion." No final conclusion was reached, though many possible reasons were given. It is not within the province of this article to recap their reasons or to offer any single explanation of my own. But reviewing some of the changes that took place on the social, economic and intellectual fronts may help to explain the radical change of mood that came about.

At the end of World War II and its aftermath, there was hope and despair in almost equal measure. While the war had brought no sense of certitude, it had the effect of affirming the triumph of good over evil. And, while the stepped-up mechanization of society seemed daily to threaten the loss of the individual's voice and will, the actual effects of security and indeed of increased affluence created a mood of hope. There was, moreover, ferment on the social scene, with increased interest in the racial question, the move to conquer poverty, and the liberation of oppressed people around the world. For the sensitive, the deeply thoughtful, the introspective man, there was the ever-increasing awareness of deadening monotony created by a mass society, awareness that the weak were defeated while the strong prevailed. This led to the questions: What were good and evil? Did they exist? And was it possible to distinguish one from the other? To counterbalance this feeling, there was a new faith in science, in the possibility of liberating mankind from the monotony of a machine existence, and the prospect of conquering the mysteries of the universe by reaching the moon.

From this seesawing of certitude and despair there came the one important influence that was to swing the tide toward hope for the future—the nearest to certitude that modern man can probably experience. That influence was the recognition of the need for a new philosophy to explain or justify the chaos of modern life. It was out of that recognition that Americans, as Frenchmen before them, turned to the philosophy of existentialism as viewed by Jean-Paul Sartre—a typical man of his age, atheistic, alienated, but desperately searching for a reason for his predicament, to make possible his will to live. Sartre's vision of a dynamic hero who created his own world of values not only allayed the threat of paralysis of will but left open the possibility of creating a new world unhampered by outworn traditions.

Yet, in the absence of any transcendent value, despair is at best held at bay, with a heroic burst of energy that is not unlike the humanist's. It was as if the writers who were using his views were themselves not fully in tune with the Sartrean blueprint. For one thing, as a transitional figure who would have to be symptomatic of society, he had to be treated ironically; but irony for the American writer who was too long fed on the tradition of romanticism was not easy to achieve. Warmth, humor, poetry—the things that make human beings distinctive as humans—kept creeping in and destroying the Sartrean figure: hence the anti-hero who straddles the two worlds of reality and romance.

There had to be a philosophical justification for the change that would take place. It was provided by another existentialist, Paul Tillich, the theologian, who represented the nonatheistic, Kierke-gaardian branch of existentialism. Like Sartre, Tillich would have no truck with the God of theism, but he had found a substitute. God, he said, is "the ground of being"; "the experience of the unconditional, the holy"—while religion is, in Tillich's favorite phrase, "ultimate concern." Religion, thus, is not a matter of dogma or morals; "There are no valid arguments for the existence of God," he explained. "But there are acts of courage in which we affirm the power of being." In practical terms, Tillich's difference from Sartre is his vision of a transcendent dimension, the religious instinct that nothing can "prove" but without which courage or the will to live (in all but the most extravagantly heroic and self-confident) is nearly impossible.

Tillich's abstract style could not affect the American people directly. His ideas had to be interpreted by a more worldly group of theologians, through books and the mass media. To "promote," as it were, a new God would mean positing again the Nietzschean cry, "God is dead!"—though this time the aim would be to show that some meaning can be salvaged outside the established authority of the church. Such books as *The Death of God* by Gabriel Vahanian, *The Secular City* by Harvey Cox, and the Rt. Rev. John Robinson's *Honest to God* (selling a million copies in England) presumed to address a post-Christian era in which a new basis of belief would be sought outside the bounds of an authoritarian God and supernatural afterworld.

It is not my task here to argue for or against these views. I would be hard-pressed indeed to establish the degree of influence they exerted on American writers. What is interesting about this ideological development is that it very closely approximates—on the surface at least—an inherent democratic tendency of American thought, reinforced by the philosophical heritage of Transcendentalism of the last century.

The offshoot of a literary-philosophical movement that lasted, all told, some fifteen years, Transcendentalism is associated with New England Puritanism and with the works of Emerson and Thoreau. But in actual fact it became the first movement in American thought that (in Emerson's words) faced "the necessity to affront the mediocrity of the time."

As a branch of Romanticism, Transcendentalism owed a major debt to the ideas that swept over Europe in the early nineteenth century. Under the impact of Carlyle and philosophical sensationalism, it turned into a rebellion against the dual orthodoxies of the Calvinist Church and the Unitarian Church of the day, which on the one hand depended on common sense and on the other viewed the dark side of man's nature. Not unlike the theology of today, the new concept at that time was that man's relation to God would have to change.

As minister of the Old North Church in Boston, Emerson had declared in a sermon that the individual did not need mediation between himself and God. Christ, he said, would have to be loved, not adored, admired by all mankind for his understanding of humanity. For this stand, he was subsequently dismissed. Six years later in his Divinity College address at Harvard, he boldly attacked the supernatural basis of Christianity, declaring it wrong to believe that revelation is something over and done with "as if God were dead."

The eloquence was all Emerson's own. But not the ideas. A "transcendental system" aiming to shake off formal restrictions on religion had begun to evolve through the auspices of a group of churchmen. In a sermon titled "Likeness to God," William Ellery Channing had written, "Our knowledge of Him comes from our own soul." Orestes Brownson, George Ripley and Frederick Henry Hodge, among others, were speculating on the theoretical relevance of Kant's idealism (Kant having been newly translated), which had created dissatisfaction in the Lockean sensationalism on which Unitarian faith rested at that time. In Kant they had found assurance that intuition, and not the senses, was the most effective source of knowledge, that "spontaneous reason" and "divine instincts" were the teachers of all truths, and that these were available to all men.

Presented thus in abstract arguments, the new philosophical insights had little chance to penetrate the contemporary consciousness. Only through literature again, through Emerson's essays, would these truths leave an indelible impression. A new surge of vitality, a dynamic, organic relationship of man to his world would now emerge, and with it the courage to take risks, to assume responsibility for one's thoughts. A general enlargement of the present moment would result from this altered perspective.

With the weakening of faith in the past, the present became more important. "The only ballast I know is respect for the present hour . . ." wrote Emerson. "We must set up the strong present tense against all rumors of wrath, past or to come."

Indeed, at some points, Emerson's essay, "Self-Reliance" resembles existential faith. "You think me a child of circumstance," he wrote in 1841. "I make my circumstances; but if you ask me whence am I, I feel like other men my relation to that Fact which cannot be spoken or defined, nor not even thought, but which exists and will exist." That fact, for Emerson, is God, who gives men the will to truth and goodness. It is his simple faith that "if we live truly, we shall see truly . . ." Thus he can minimize evil and emphasize the positive.

If we turn again to the novelists mentioned earlier, we can hear distinct echoes of the transcendental faith in their works. In his novels and stories, John Updike's characters appear to be searching for an inner vision that will make life meaningful. Though they are not models of virtue, are often gauche and socially unreliable, they are in a sense redeemed by an inner craving for something to believe in. What one realizes is that the hero's irresponsibility is not against himself but against society which has let him down. "All I know is what's inside of me. That's all I have," he confesses; and to the minister who asks if he believes in God, he answers, "Goodness lies inside; there is nothing outside." What he wants and needs is the experience of affirmation.

Though Malamud's *The Fixer* is not one of his more original novels, it serves an another example of the transcendental trend. How unlike the Emerson image, you will say, is Yakov Bak, the penniless Jewish handyman in pre-Revolutionary Russia who is framed by the government. Yakov states how he feels when confronting the Investigating Magistrate. "God and nature are one and the same and so is man. If you understand that a man's mind is part of God, then you understand it as well as I. In that way you are free, if you are in the mind of God." When faced with an unjust fate, he simply affirms: "One thing I've learned, there is no such thing as a nonpolitical man." Unfortunately, this message is somehow lost on the reader because the novel does not really seem to demonstrate this message. How can one be sure that had Yakov been a political man he would have been saved?

In his early stories, Salinger seemed to be groping toward a mystical vision, a transcendent moment when life becomes suddenly meaningful: but usually loss has reached a point of no return. In "Uncle Wiggily in Connecticut," there is a feeling of lost innocence; in "De Daumier-Smith's Blue Period," there is a sense of spiritual identity, a search for detachment—"everybody is a nun" is how the hero sums it up. After those stories Salinger seemed for a while to be veering toward a Zen-Buddhist faith. But in *Franny and Zooey* (1961), he has discovered a different spirituality. When Franny comes home from college for the holidays looking as if she were on the verge of a breakdown and/or spiritual conversion, Zooey, who acts like a spiritual catalyst on others, decides it is time for Franny to learn the meaning of true faith—not the ersatz variety she has picked up from the so-called religious books, one of which she clutches in her hands, written in the last century by a Russian mystic. Christ becomes the leading figure in his teaching, for, as Zooey explains to her: "Who besides Jesus knew . . . that we're carrying the Kingdom of Heaven around with us, *inside* where we're all too goddam stupid and sentimental and unimaginative to look?" The religious thing to do is to *act*. From Christ, Zooey has learned humility—we're all important in this world.

But while Salinger's faith seems closer to the faith of the church and the teaching of Christ, Saul Bellow's is a faith for men who need to know that life is possibility. His worldly egomaniacs would hardly qualify as "religious" in the accepted meaning of the word. An inherent restlessness, an unwillingness, in the last analysis, to conform, drives them to examine what is lacking in their lives. In one novel, *Seize the Day,* for instance, the message becomes "the wisdom of seizing the life within us . . . the need not to die." The same kind of will power keeps another unsaintly Augie March from defeat. As he puts it: "I have a feeling about the axial lines of life, with respect to which you must be straight or else your existence is merely clownery, hiding tragedy . . . . when striving stops, there they are as a gift: Truth, Love, Peace, Bounty, Usefulness, Harmony."

But it is Herzog who best expresses the transcendental faith that vacillates between a kind of intellectual weariness of struggle and a childlike eagerness to begin anew. He writes to a friend who has written a paper on "Interpretations of Suffering" based on Kierkegaard:

"Let us set aside the fact that such convictions in the mouths of safe, comfortable people, playing at crisis, alienation, apocalypse, desperation, make me sick. We must get it out of our heads that . . . we are waiting for the end . . . . the advocacy and praise of suffering take us in the wrong direction, and those of us who remain loyal to civilization must not go for it." What he would like to substitute for this kind of negation is a form of spontaneous faith. ". . . When you see what strange notions, hallucinations, projections, issue from the human mind you begin to believe in Providence again. To survive these idiocies . . . . Anyway, the intellectual has been a Separatist. And what kind of synthesis is a Separatist likely to come up with? Lucky for me I didn't have the means to get too far from our common life. I'm glad of that. I mean to share with other human beings as far as possible and not destroy my remaining years in the same way."

1967

The Multiform American Imagination

A young Indian novelist, speaking perfect English, recently confronted me with the question: Why were the newest American novelists so difficult to like and understand? Why, when he appreciated Hemingway, Faulkner (about whom he was writing a book), Steinbeck and even Bellow, did he find it hard to respond to such writers as Jack Kerouac, William Burroughs, John Barth . . . he reeled off the names with some uncertainty. Because the question didn't have a quick answer and our meeting had to be short, I passed on the task of answering it to Tony Tanner, whose new book on American fiction was conveniently lying on my desk in the *Sunday Book Review* office. I had not read it yet but had confidence in Mr. Tanner as a young English critic whose interpretations of American literature combine the astuteness of V. S. Pritchett with the adventuresomeness of Anthony Burgess.

The Multiform American Imagination

Having now read *City of Words,* I can add that Mr. Tanner is not only adept at interpreting our literature but also remarkably gifted at explaining what it means to be an American novelist at midcentury. Physical distance has given him perspective, but beyond that a mental habit of synthesis and definition has enabled him to grapple at the same time with the multifarious works of some twenty-five writers now in the limelight and with the still-elusive shape of the new American imagination. His engagement with the postmoderns is less provocative than Leslie Fiedler's and less judicious than Richard Poirier's, but it contains the enthusiasm of someone who has "discovered" something for himself. And nothing makes a book more readable.

Using no biographical data and confining background material to appendices, he plunges directly into the novels and stories themselves, taking each writer separately yet continuously making cross-references as he extracts from the works what he considers to be their common intent. Whether the voice is Saul Bellow's in *Mr. Sammler's Planet* or James Purdy's in *Cabot Wright Begins* ("one of the most important novels since the war"), Norman Mailer's in *An American Dream,* or Kurt Vonnegut, Jr.'s in an early story, *Player Piano,* the concern always centers, Mr. Tanner shows, on a particular American dilemma: "that of finding enough form not to be a mere jelly, but not so much form that one is fixed once and for all within a defining shape." On the one hand, endless references to "jelly," "jelly-fish" and "clay" reveal the writer's (and his hero's) dread of formlessness, invisibility; on the other hand, recurring images of screens and mirrors suggest his anxiety toward deadening patterns and systems. A key concept he finds is "entropy," the feeling that everything is running down.

It is the special quality of the experience and not the experience itself that is new, and what sustains our interest throughout his unrelenting documentation is the dimension he adds to the old cliché of the picaresque hero. In pointing out the anti-hero's moral ambiguity, his deviousness and mocking flexibility, little has been said up to now about that innermost impulse—paranoia—that drives him, not to alienation, but to re-creation. In Mr. Tanner's book, we see him seeking shelter not from bombs but from self-annihilation in a spiritually polluted world, exploring the City of Words (an image borrowed from Nabokov's cunning allegory *Pale Fire*)—a fictive landscape propelled solely by the imagination. The "prisons of the self" that Nabokov's characters experience, the alternating sense of revulsion and void in the work of Burroughs and Barth, Vonnegut's and Pynchon's metaphoric islands and planets—all attest to a metaphysical engagement that belies a surface cynicism. From that vantage point, Mr. Tanner's uniform admiration of the new writers becomes understandable.

But intent is one thing and achievement another, and Mr. Tanner's method does not work so well when it comes to assessing what he has observed from a single angle. His dependence on a general scheme (ironically, what his writers all fear) tends to blur the novelist's individual character, his art, his tone. The discussion begins to sound like a cover story for *Time*, all strands mishmashed for easier digestion and export. With only oblique references to style, the writers seem almost interchangeable. Yet the withering wasteland of *Naked Lunch,* flooding the reader's consciousness with its cumulative effects, is patently saying something quite different from the emotionally charged world of the Invisible Man, poised between explosion and revelation.

If anything emerges at the end from the juxtaposition of dissimilar styles—from the savage expressionism of John Hawkes (in *The Cannibal*) to the quasi-mysticism of John Updike's earlier work—it is that the American imagination is far from uniform. Its flexibility makes possible today two opposing tendencies (sometimes confused in a writer's work)—the existential strain, still mostly humanistic, which links writers like Bellow, Ellison, Malamud and Roth to the previous generation of writers, and a more contemporary strain of fantasy that derives from surrealist, expressionist and neo-realist modes. Having shed their social skins, this latter group of writers seems prepared to shed their "human natures." Before a brutal, gaudy, absurd, dehumanized environment, their dark laughter is ominous and unforgiving. When their art matches their visions (as in Nabokov and Borges), they remind us of those disenchanted post-Elizabethans who saw evil in the very nature of things. But Mr. Tanner would have to agree that most of the time the shock these writers deal our senses is therapeutic rather than purging.

1971

Unwilling Ironists

An unbiased review of Ihab Hassan's *Radical Innocence* must begin with admiration for the conception of his book. Forsaking all others (those tempting early moderns), he has chosen to embrace that much maligned, barely examined stepchild of modern criticism: the contemporary American novel. "The postmoderns," as he calls Carson McCullers, Saul Bellow, J. D. Salinger, and some forty other writers of their vintage, have reason to feel flattered by the serious concern that has impelled him to fill a whole book with criticism of their work, all of it informed, exuberant, and sympathetic. A closely reasoned, somewhat academic approach has not prevented him, moreover, from taking a firm stand: namely, that "American fiction is not a mean or shabby spectacle" but rather life-enhancing, helping us (as Lawrence claimed for the novel at its best) "not to be a dead man in life." Whatever the extent of Mr. Hassan's success in this respect, his commitment has forced an essential critical effort: the search for a viable bond between the life and the literature of our day.

Without awareness of such a bond, there can be no real criticism of the contemporary novel, only remonstrations. The negativism of critics to the new in art is an old story, but the postwar generation of American writers has also had problems uniquely its own. Constituting no single school and presenting no immediately striking point of view, they have had no spokesman, no Alain (*Nouveau Roman*) Robbe-Grillet, no John (Angry Young Man) Osborne. If anything, they have learned from Hemingway to throw the critics off the scent—something easy enough to do, considering the violence and sensationalism which characterize their work. The literal-minded critic and the critic of refined taste have suffered equally from the new novel's long day's journey into nightmare. In the absence of visible values, there remained only to impute unworthy motives to the writer: himself debased, he must drag the reader down to his own level. In the final analysis, the dissenting critic would rather explain away American fiction than contend with the dark image of America that it seems to him to reflect.

To this restrictive view, Mr. Hassan's interesting study is a salutary corrective. Whatever the limitations of his own approach, he has taken the leap which makes possible the shifting of blame from the writer to the reader—who has simply not seen what is there. With good sense and an aesthetic awareness that generally restrains his tendency to go off into abstraction, he directs us to the form of the novel, reminding us how basically meaning is controlled by it. The premise of the modern novel as an artistic entity whose values are *created* and therefore subject to interpretation is as old as Henry James. What has added to the complexity and confusion of the new novel, Mr. Hassan contends, is the impact of a new social reality—man's changing relation to his environment. In an elaborately structured exposition, he traces the two visible effects of this change—the emergence of a new, morally ambiguous hero (the anti-hero, so-called), and the blurring of contours between illusion and truth. At the source of this change, he suggests, is an *existential* orientation whose signature is irony.

Mr. Hassan relates this attitude, or philosophy, to a significant American trait he calls "radical innocence"—an extravagant hopefulness and faith in the future that in effect negate evil and death. He shows that this correlative of the American Dream has been increasingly at variance with the values of a destructive, overorganized society before which the individual begins by feeling helpless and ends by becoming indifferent. Poised between "radical innocence" and "experience," the new hero weighs the advantages of "rebellion" through "recoil" and, after a painful "initiation," accepts the role of "victim" to escape "reconciliation" with "the dead social center."

The quick summary in the last sentence is not meant to suggest the quality of the author's thought (which always attempts to be thorough) but the quality of his style, which abounds in dialectic and metaphor. In addition, readers may be put off by his lapses into terminology borrowed from the pseudo-sciences and Aristotle (by way of Northrop Frye). But if the mannerisms of his style tend generally to complicate his meaning, they also help to release apt images that make concision and synthesis possible:

> Between nihilism and sainthood, the modern self wavers, seeking still the meaning of life. In its concrete encounter with absurdity, with dread and the obscene corporeality of death, with mystical anarchy and organized nothingness, with abstract truth and experienced reality, the modern self discovers ways of affirmation that heroes of yore did not envision.

Having defined "recoil" as "a way of taking a stand . . . a strategic retreat into self," Mr. Hassan is able to relate meaningfully the quixotic youths of Salinger, the "defeated" heroes of William Styron, and Bernard Malamud's ludicrous misfits. They are all, even Mailer's self-made psychopaths and Ellison's Invisible Man, reflections of "the victim with a thousand faces" whose experiences demonstrate "the sharpening of polarity between Self and the World." It is this separation that is leading the contemporary novel away from straightforward realism into the special world of irony where "distortion is moral judgment, perversity, criticism."

So long as the emphasis remains on the ideas themselves, Mr. Hassan's comparisons prove stimulating, his conclusions persuasive. But when he begins to document his generalized portrait of the hero with lengthier investigations from a wide range of current novels, he forces us to look more closely at certain oft-repeated terms, and in doing so we note their ambiguous usage.

Two of his key words, "existential" and "ironic," prove especially troublesome. Though he identifies "the new awareness" as "largely existential," adding, with caution, "the existential pattern implies a view of life that may be traced to Job," his understanding of what lifts the most subterranean anti-hero to stature and dignity bears little affinity to the "grandeur in despair" of Camus and even less to the more simple patience of Job. The term "irony," on the other hand, is simply overworked. Flashed like a spotlight on each novel to ferret hidden meaning, it eventually reveals its uneven usefulness as a form to novelists who lack the basic discipline of skepticism on which true irony subsists. And, while one admires the complex scheme by which he relates three variants of irony (near tragedy, tragicomedy, and comedy) to three corresponding aspects of the anti-hero (the scapegoat, the humble hero, the rogue), one finds little usefulness in the end in the juxtaposition of such dissimilar novels as *The Naked and the Dead, A Long Day's Journey,* and *The Ginger Man.*

But it is in the final section, devoted to "the individual talent," that the theories more perceptibly begin to pale. Though Mr. Hassan brings considerable insight to his discussion of the four especially gifted writers he has singled out—McCullers, Capote, Salinger, and

Bellow—he seems curiously impervious to the final implication of their more positive accent, to what he himself defines as "the need to overcome the condition of recoil and seek reconciliation between self and the world."

Suffering and endurance are the ironical substance of Mrs. Mc-Cullers's tragedies of unrequited love, as he points out, but tempering her irony with wistfulness is her gentle knowledge that love defines and makes the fragmented individual whole. In the same way, to stress the "narcissistic impulse of Capote's fiction" is to miss the final pathos of his world within world in which the quest for self becomes identified with the need to establish contact with others, and through them with reality. Mr. Hassan apparently recognizes the quixotic gesture in Salinger as a sign of "faith in the willingness of the spirit," but he does not connect this with the search for detachment that leads at last (in *Franny and Zooey*) to religious vision. And, turning finally to Bellow, what is it that his insatiable adventurer-individualists betray at the end if not the sobering knowledge that freedom without a personal commitment to others is self-defeating? Mr. Hassan only hints at this.

What is forcefully brought home to the reader (if not to Mr. Hassan) is how closely reconciliation is linked in these writers to *transcendence* (indeed, even Ellison's Invisible Man ends up by affirming "the principle"), with faith in the ideal, the abstract. And, while this weakens the revolt of the unconditioned, *existential* self, it appears to strengthen the capacity of the *essential* self to envision Truth. There is a sense of fatality at the source of existentialism that in the last analysis links it with determinism. It is because these writers defy equally the destructive element in society and the limits of human destiny that they often prove unwilling ironists. In their insistence on the redeeming power of love, on the almost mystical need to connect with others and to preserve the self's inner truth, they reveal a spiritual dimension that belies the surface negativism of their work.

Whether or not their initial impulse is existential, as Mr. Hassan suggests, the resolution of this impulse, in at least four writers, appears to draw them close to an older life-enhancing tradition—the classical American novel. There is enough evidence in Mr. Hassan's book to stimulate readers in sympathy with this view to enlarge upon it.

1962

PART TWO

Three Post-Psychological
Novels

When in 1925, Ortega y Gasset, in his *The Dehumanization of Art and Notes on the Novel* was spreading gloom about the future of modern fiction, it was no doubt hard to take seriously his prediction that a dead end awaited the psychological novel. In Proust's prodigious work he saw the ultimate paralysis that would result from a microscopic analysis of the human soul, and he foresaw the day when psychology would become such common knowledge that its fictional treatment would pall. And from there, where could the novel go? With little enough left to invent in terms of plot, there seemed to him to be only one remaining path for the novel—the depiction of an "imaginary psychology." But Ortega left the term only hazily defined, skeptical perhaps that this was something possible to achieve.

From our present vantage point it is easy to see that the Spanish critic's pessimism was exaggerated: Proust was far from being the beginning of the end. Yet Ortega was not entirely mistaken about the abuses the psychological novel would suffer. The subtleties of a technique intended for a self-conscious inward probing, in the hands of the nonartist, could turn into mere platitudes of the clinical case study. Not that such distortion could in itself lead to the psychological novel's undoing. A literary technique exists to support a particular vision of reality, and its usefulness is not spent while the validity of that vision remains unchallenged.

Slowly, inevitably, the challenge has come. Inward turning cannot become habit-forming in a world where man's privacy is increasingly invaded, and as our system of associations becomes more complex, self-identity is harder than ever to achieve. What price remembrance of things past when, in Jean-Paul Sartre's words, "there is no reality except in action"? "We live not in depth but flatly," Gertrude Stein had asserted even earlier, suggesting that our consciousness of reality was contained wholly in the present moment. Since the days of the early Hemingway, with his desire to learn "what really happened in action . . . what produced the emotion you experienced," a tradition has been building to lay bare man's integral connection with the tangible world, to establish his presence through his response to the moment's unfolding experience.

From France comes word of a new school, variously called "la littérature du regard," "l'alittérature" and "le nouveau réalisme." It appears that the French are catching up in a big way with the hitherto barely publicized trend of the post-psychological novel. In France, where the writer is always more articulate and more easily given to theorizing than his British or American counterpart, a group of novelists has demonstrated, manifesto-style, the advantages of the new manner. Going all out, writers like Alain Robbe-Grillet, Michel Butor and Marguerite Duras claimed to be destroying not only the naturalistic trappings of the novel but the Proust-inspired encumbrances of symbolism as well.

Among these, a Russian-born woman, Nathalie Sarraute,* is probably the most durable talent. In three ambitious novels written within ten years, she has sought to a fanatical degree to discredit the psychological novel of the Proustian school. In *Portrait of a Man Unknown* (which caused a stir in French critical circles), her first novel to reach us in translation, she seeks to demonstrate the theories she set forth in a much-discussed essay, "The Era of Suspicion." Introducing

---

*Mme. Sarraute's eighth novel, *Fools Say*, was published in 1977.

us to Mme. Sarraute, Jean-Paul Sartre applauds her for writing an "anti-novel," one that resists the traditional premises of plot and character. But before American readers can echo M. Sartre's enthusiasm, they will probably have to overcome an initial response of bewilderment, exasperation and even revulsion.

For this is essentially an unpleasant little novel in which life is made to seem disturbingly amorphous and characters have little more substance than the featureless faces in a de Chirico painting. Physically undefined, or only barely sketched in, the characters are, moreover, nameless and with only the vaguest hint of a past life. Our conception of the two major figures, an elderly man and his spinster daughter, is dependent wholly on the extravagant imagination of the narrator, a self-confessed neurotic who feels disassociated from his surroundings. As a neighbor, he takes every opportunity to snoop and eavesdrop on the pair, and though they have no real relation to him, he develops a deep antagonism toward them which he takes pleasure in communicating.

The drabness and meanness of their existence oppresses him. He views them against a background of "damp little courtyards," of narrow, smelly corridors, and he comes to associate them with the rows of identical houses bordered by "wan little gravel plots" where men and women sit idly for hours. Behind the hearty, forced friendliness of the old man, the narrator perceives a fanatical miser with a brutish will to dominate; the daughter, on the other hand, he feels sure, masks a weak, dependent nature behind a self-righteous, martyred front. Secretly witnessing their petty tricks of mutual bondage, overhearing their continual quarrels over money, their sententious self-justifications before neighbors, the narrator sees them gradually divested of all human dignity.

His descriptions of them become, significantly, full of similes of slimy, crawling creatures. The father is "like a huge spider, watching and waiting . . . the entire universe like a web of his own weaving." The daughter, taken by surprise, "squirms . . . weak and defenseless as a hermit crab just taken out of its shell." He catches them confronting each other "with their snake-like coiling and uncoiling" or "like two enormous dung-beetles." They are endless, these references to crabs, snakes, insects—creatures activated by the simplest kind of reflex.

What does it all mean? Is it mere hallucination, or is there behind the narrator's Kafkaesque self-torment a groping toward some larger truth? We soon see that despite his abnormal obsession, the man is no fool. There are hints of a lonely, ailing childhood spent in quiet observation; and subtle references to Rilke, Baudelaire and Dostoevsky suggest that he is also well read. He has always been conscious of a conventional, playacting humanity: "women, very proper, with trim hats . . . refastening their gloves before ringing the door bell"; young girls "watching and waiting on plush chairs at dancing class or in ballrooms or in casinos at fashionable resorts"; young men (their easy preys) "with the same airy supple way of holding their heads . . . . the tentacles that issued already from the girls, the little sucking, groping valves, hardly grazed them." And, finally, he has seen the girls build their "soft little nests . . . from bits and scraps"—from books, plays, songs, proverbs "they spin their cocoon, their impermeable covering." Thus they have become at last the cliché-bound, collective "they," the conforming social being.

The narrator's habit of spying, we discover, involves an anxiety about the nature of reality that is akin to the artist's concern. He has discovered that people in their ordinary everyday relations cannot disengage the mask of the social being from the authentic self: "each one of them appears to us as a finished, perfect whole, entirely enclosed on every side, a solid, hard block, without a single fissure." It is in order to penetrate this "hard block" that he has sought to develop a sixth sense about people. Yet he confesses that all he has found is "a shapeless, gray covering from which all blood has been drained away."

With the persistence of a sleuth, he awaits the final explosion: the ultimate confrontation of father and daughter over the question of a loan which the woman needs for medical care. In that moment of unconditional refusal and mutual incrimination there stands exposed the tremendous force of an intimacy that has behind it nothing but social conditioning; dependent upon each other, they have never felt love, only self-interest. This is the one tangible happening in the novel, and it is especially effective for being played against the final scene—a kind of coda. With the daughter finally married and out of his way, the old man is suddenly "all played out" and the narrator becomes "normal" at last, satisfied, like the rest of the community, to live off ordinary local gossip. Now that the objects of his curiosity have a past that he knows, there is nothing left to explore, to imagine, to construct.

Here is a reversal of the Proustian theme: in Mme. Sarraute's novel nothing leads us to the past; in fact, knowledge of the past seems to impair the process of perception. The facet of human nature that interests this writer is too elusive for the traditional method of the psychological analysis. What we have had revealed are not the broad outlines of behavior but the minute actions of the autonomic nervous system which seeks to maintain an equilibrium between itself and its immediate surroundings. This spontaneous response of the organism (Mme. Sarraute in another novel, *Tropismes,* has likened it to the action of plants) is one which builds through the individual's rubbing up against the common denominator of society. When we complain that Mme. Sarraute has not created character in this novel, we miss the point that she has tried to make: that in the leveling process of society, character is not easily "created." Mme. Sarraute's success at the end—and it is a success of a kind—depends chiefly on the intensity of her vision and her poetic insights, both of which are considerable.

Neither in its characters nor in its setting does Ivy Compton-Burnett's *A Father and His Fate* resemble *Portrait of a Man Unknown,* yet the two novels have something essentially in common. Here, in the drawing room of an Edwardian country-house, is the same flat world of externally manifested values in which the individual cannot possibly survive. In the nineteen novels Miss Compton-Burnett has published since 1925, she has quietly been evolving a style all her own. One might call it revolutionary, for the novel has seen nothing like it. Eliminating almost all description and all comment on character and situation, she has contrived to make her novels read like plays—for they are nearly all dialogue. But with this difference: no characters in a play have ever been known to speak as hers do—with not a shred of inhibition. Never introduced, they simply appear, and for the duration of the novel they never cease talking.

And how they talk! All the words are double-edged, brilliant, arched, and in the final instance mortally wounding. They say in the same breath what is expected of them and what lies so deeply buried in them that they are themselves unaware what their words expose. Just as for Sartre's characters there is no reality except in action, so for Miss Compton-Burnett's there is no reality except in the spoken word. It is through these words alone that we enter into her characters' minds.

As in her other novels, one's first impression here is that her men and women are compensating with "serpent's tongue" for the loss of something fundamentally precious. Again, the family is the arena in which the individual is victimized. The titles alone of her novels reveal the source of conflict that interests her: *Brothers and Sisters, Men and Wives, A House and Its Head, Mother and Son.* In the present novel, the father, Miles, is a tragicomic Lear figure, a tyrannous humbug, dependent on the family's flattery and insidiously bent on asserting his authority by thought-control of those around him. Untroubled by a conscience, he attends to his needs as they arise: "I live in the present, I give myself up to the present," he confesses.

And we see that this is true: he is no sooner widowed than he plans remarriage, openly stealing his nephew's young fiancée from under his nose. Later, when his wife returns (her death had been a false rumor), he quickly readjusts, rationalizing his actions without the least discomposure. Supported by his five o'clock tea, the speechless presence of the servants and the ready-made expressions that see him through any of life's ordeals, he never allows the serenity of the moment to be disturbed, whatever the cost in moral terms, in betrayal, in loss of trust.

Here, more patently than in Mme. Sarraute's novel, we observe the disastrous consequences of social conditioning, which Miss Compton-Burnett views mainly in a ludicrous light. The three daughters, Constance, Ursula and Audrey, have been so protected from the outside world that even the desire to break free through marriage has not occurred to them. So they exist like bric-a-brac, doing apparently nothing, pointlessly talking and arguing, especially with a male cousin who plies them with cynical thoughts. Their sentiments, their inmost thoughts (which they never keep to themselves) do not match their actions. They act nobly and conventionally but speak crudely and rebelliously. To lash out, Hamlet-like, at their closest opponent at the point where he is weakest is their only way of asserting their identity. Thus, when Miles asks his daughters, "I wonder if there is anyone who cares for me. I often ask myself that question," Ursula answers vengefully: "Then you should answer it. It is less safe to put it to other people." They are quick with retorts that aim to deflate their father.

Yet in the midst of this bitter and brittle dialogue there is more than a suggestion of the tragedy that is the other side of the coin. There is a kind of pathos in the vacillation the girls suffer between what they think they are and what they have become. When news of their mother's death reaches them, true to their upbringing, they give no outward sign of weakness. Audrey alone gives vent to bitterness, when, told she is not her real self, she replies: "This is my real self. What is not natural is to show it. . . . We show the selves we are accustomed to show and other people to expect. . . . You show the one you have come to think is yours."

There is in Miss Compton-Burnett's conception of man vs. English society a larger-than-life reality, an implied horror that, despite her extreme melodramatic situations, leaves an unforgettable impression.

Elizabeth Montagu, a more recent and younger post-psychological novelist, has attracted attention in England on the strength of two prior novels and a number of short stories. It is very likely that her short, skillful third novel, *This Side of the Truth,* will be underestimated in this country or at best praised for the wrong reasons. It is unfortunately part of our reviewing tradition to lump novels into easy categories by subject matter, and this one unluckily seems to fall into that much overcrowded niche of "life as seen through the eyes of a sensitive child." Yet, as she herself disclaims in an author's note, this is not meant to be a realistic portrayal of a thirteen-year-old girl. She has set out only "to give an impression . . . . at the age of 13 one lives in a strange kind of country which appears to lie between what one has been and what one is about to become."

At first glance, indeed, Miss Montagu's Sarah (who is the narrator) seems a close copy of Carson McCullers's Frankie Addams, a lonely child bewildered by the actions of a grown-up world that will not let her "belong." Though leading a much more sophisticated life than Frankie, she states her position at one point in much the same way: "I nearly am grown up and hate missing things." Yet this is one of the few directly revealing statements she makes. For Miss Montagu is not writing the stream-of-consciousness novel in which the character's own awareness is our guide. Taken in their literal sense, Sarah's spoken thoughts are at best false clues. For her real intent, her unconscious desire, we must look to the actions or *implied actions* which inadvertently result.

The only child of divorced parents, victim of the whims of an unstable mother who has been remarried, to a man much younger than herself, Sarah conceives of herself as an innocent bystander in a world of strangely behaving adults. Although she pretends to have no particular bias toward anyone, she gives herself away by what she observes and the manner in which she observes it. At the French Riviera, on vacation with her mother and stepfather, Mark, she becomes entangled (through her own masked intentions) with two other houseguests, the "beautiful" Catherine and her "disagreeable" fiancé, Mr. Kaplan. Led on first by simple curiosity, she is guided by her intuition to the heart of a situation which involves her stepfather and ultimately brings about the breach that has been building between her mother and herself.

Sarah's resentment of her mother, at first only vaguely sensed by casual remarks, becomes more noticeable as she sides with Mark against her mother over Mark's obvious attraction to Catherine. From bits and fragments ("that is what mother is always doing, spoiling things") the portrait is fixed of a snobbish, dishonest, unloving, frigid and neurotic woman who has been closely watched by her daughter with something less than love or even tolerance.

On the other hand, one can see that Mark means more to Sarah than she can yet understand or is willing to admit. For he enters her thoughts all too often and unexpectedly. To draw closer to Mark she maneuvers to take Catherine into her confidence.

But there is still more here than meets the eye. Sarah's curiosity, we gradually realize, has a deeper intent. Watching Catherine's window at night from her room ("I wasn't spying or anything; I often stood there. I just liked to watch her in her room"), like Mme. Sarraute's narrator, she has "the feeling of things happening." Her innocence becomes suspect when she pretends to be asleep in order to hear a private conversation between Catherine and Mr. Kaplan that involves Mark. We realize that she is up to something when, to hide her snooping from her mother, she pretends to have been sleepwalking. Is it vengeance on her mother she is plotting, or is this mere diabolical mischief in the manner of the natural children in a de la Mare story?

There is the suggestion of both in her tantalizing reply to her suspicious mother when questioned about what she has seen: "Oh, nothing in particular. . . . I knew what she was doing: she was trying to read my mind: I lay and thought of nothing." After that one watches Sarah with apprehension as she stalks Mark's path, unconscious of her own needs and undeclared intentions. One suspects it will take a catastrophe, as in fact it does, to finally fix adult awareness of responsibility in Sarah.

This is not an easy story to follow; viewed through Sarah's partial eyes, facts are mingled with fancy. The actions of the characters remain puzzling not only to the child but to the reader. Thus it is hard to know where Sarah's faulty imagination begins and the author's own limitations end. Like Mme. Sarraute and Miss Compton-Burnett, Miss Montagu has not set out to reveal these characters to us as individuals; like them what interests her is our constantly changing relation to the "truth."

Have these three novels really abandoned psychology? To suggest this would be quite misleading. Their authors are obviously still concerned with how and why people act as they do. What they have wanted to avoid is the usual "analysis," the logic of cause and effect which must guide the interpretation of recognized forms of behavior. There has been a clear shift from the Jamesian ideal of awareness. Moving into the murky area of purely organic being (which all but unconsciously adjusts to the social mold), the writer has discovered a new direction for the novel. Since in a changing world we remain in a constant state of flux, only our actions and words can give proof of what we really are. Hence our increasing dependence on objective reality, on *felt experience.*

The novel is beginning to read like a detective story in which the reader is asked to search out the truth about human beings within an "imaginary psychology" such as Ortega probably envisioned. It is a fascinating search so long as the idea of the individual is not destroyed. Unfortunately this threat is great in the three novels here considered. The authors, three intelligent, sensitive women, have not quite succeeded in convincing us that the novel can survive without character or that character can be disengaged from the individual.

1958

A Writer and Her Vision: Ivy Compton-Burnett

Devotees of Ivy Compton-Burnett (they must be numerous enough to form a society) are familiar by now with the standard publicity handout that shows the novelist as every inch the dour Victorian schoolmarm. Looks were never more deceiving. Dame Ivy, who died at the age of eighty-five, after finishing her twentieth novel, is, in fact, a revolutionary figure in modern literature. With a magic all her own, for the last half century she has broken through the conventions of fiction to turn the English comedy of manners into a stunning parody of itself. I find it curious that the subversive element of her vision—what one might call her anti-Establishmentism—has so far escaped her English critics, who tend to regard her as only a slightly more waspish Austenesque interpreter of the human comedy. Like Jane Austen's, of course, her series of novels (set in Edwardian England at the beginning of the century) has unity of time and place, and like hers it deals with the landed gentry. But a dissimilarity of intent suggests itself to me in the modern novelist's disregard for texture in contrast to Miss Austen's carefully wrought regionalism. Dame Ivy's novels are, in fact, descriptively bare: Like the abstractionist painter, she depends on the telling stroke (one dare not skip a word in her slim novels). Her major innovation—narration through conversation—leaves the author no opportunity to comment directly on the action, to moralize. Static figures in a landscape, her characters are revealed by what they say, not by what they do or think.

And what double-edged words their serpents' tongues let loose, what unspeakable compulsions their *consciousness* lays bare! Over the surface serenity of the breakfast table (where the action usually begins) a bitter residue of festering wounds mingles with chitchat about how to cut the ham. The human comedy with its variety of types and motivations has narrowed down to a "human nature" whose chief component is the will to power. As the very titles of Dame Ivy's novels testify, power struggle is her theme: *Brothers and Sisters, Men and Wives, A House and Its Head, Mother and Son,* etc. But the violence that results—murder, incest, theft, betrayal, any action, in fact, inspired by cold hatred and callousness—is in itself less interesting than what we see revealed as the inner sources of power and the ultimate effect it has on those who live in its shadow.

At the center of the stage, inevitably, is the Family, a microcosm of the Corporate Society, circumscribed by its national, political, cultural and even linguistic habits. So binding are its regulations and regularity that when a member attempts to fly the coop, an invisible hand promptly reaches out to reclaim him. Chance plays a large role in these dramatic novels, where the individual's will to freedom must at the last bend to the collective Will. In *The Last and the First*, as in her other novels, power changes hands with the slightest of alteration for all concerned. The Queen is dead, long live . . .

The reigning tyrant of this comparatively temperate novel (for Dame Ivy) is fifty-five-year-old Eliza, known as Mater. Her subjects are an aging, adoring husband, Sir Robert; and four grown children, two of whom are Sir Robert's by a previous marriage. Without scruple, she opens their mail, dictates their friendships, lectures them on the priority of manners over feelings. Autocrat with a martyr complex, she is convinced that she can do only good: "But the yoke is not always easy or the burden light," she complains in the axiom of her day. (The novel abounds in axiomatic clichés: conditioned reflexes that resist thought.)

The rebel in her path is the stepdaughter Hermia, who at thirty-four realizes that she must "go out into the world." Her innocence long shed, she is clear-eyed, ironical and unforgiving toward Eliza. When she makes known her desire to leave home and join forces with the headmistress of a local school to save the school from bankruptcy, she not only sets off a verbal explosion between herself and Eliza but also alerts the other children to the facts of family life—the shape of things to come.

They respond as children of their time. High-minded, Pollyannish Madeline speaks in even more banal accents than her mother: "No one can do much in daily life. We simply do our best in the sphere that happens to be ours." Decadently witty Angus, the youngest, takes no sides, preferring to mock what others unsuitably sanctify. Only Roberta, who has the making of a Shavian heroine, has the paradoxical turn of mind to counter answers with questions: "Is simple openness really the best in everything?"

If the children are the Chorus who surface undercurrents, the servants and neighbors are Public Opinion: the seal and stamp of patterned thought. Unctuous and obtrusive, the "lower orders" have learned to wield a power of their own: they are the traffic controllers of gossip and family secrets between households. In this instance, Hermia's news turns out to be of particular interest to another neighboring autocrat, eighty-four-year-old Jocasta, who is desperate for a prospective heir. Having held her power through a gushing benevolence, she has produced a fawning, ineffectual son and (inadvertently) encouraged a brood of parasitical grandchildren. Her eagerness to meet the "heroic" Hermia is motivated by a need to mortgage the family's future.

With typical irony, and melodrama verging on the absurd, Hermia's wheel of fortune turns about. A large inheritance from a virtual stranger falls into her lap just as Eliza declares the family's financial ruin. With a sudden proposal of marriage from Jocasta's son adding to her sense of security, Hermia turns lady bountiful, giving her fortune away to family and friends. Like the denouement of a Shakespearean comedy, Hermia's reign is secured in an atmosphere of general forgiveness, and harmony prevails in Cinderella land. But only for a moment.

Before the final curtain, the children return frontstage with their life-negating refrains: "Let us put it out of our minds . . . let us not think or talk of it. . . ." They have glimpsed "real life" where love and trust are dead, and they cannot face it. In Dame Ivy's final vision there looms again the dread of a clinging moribund past that blocks all exits to the future.

1971

Carson McCullers:
Love Perverse and Perfect

There was no clock on the freshly painted mantelpiece of Carson McCullers's living room—only two crystalline candlesticks with long white candles. Dressed all in white down to her spotless tennis shoes, the celebrated Southern novelist—almost a recluse of late—rose from her armchair to greet her visitor. There was a moment's stillness. Then, through the doorway, broadly smiling, came Ida, white uniform against dark skin, all cheer and solicitude, holding a brightly decorated vest, like a chasuble, for "Sister" to wear. Unobtrusively present as she served the drinks, Ida spoke the lines that recalled us to time and the business of living.

In her mid-forties, Carson McCullers still looked like a frail growing girl. With her closely cropped brown hair, gray-blue eyes that looked straight at you, and a gentle voice tinged with the South, she seemed at first like a precocious child who had been called away from a higher plane of being. The impression was fleeting. Alongside the slightly brooding, vulnerable "young" look there lurked a quick, teasing humor and philosophic calm. There was an aura of timeless serenity in her spacious Victorian-gothic house in Nyack, New York, where for more than two decades she had fought ill health, fear of sudden death, and physical incapacity. The latter had repeatedly threatened to obliterate her writing career and finally condemned her to a wheelchair. After her husband's death in 1953 she had remained in the house alone except for her nurse-housekeeper, Ida.

This was a far cry from the informal literary salon of the Brooklyn brownstone over which Mrs. McCullers had presided in the early years of her fame as the twenty-two-year-old prodigy author of *The Heart Is a Lonely Hunter.* But she did not dwell on it. She had just finished her first novel in nine years, *Clock Without Hands* (about racial tension in the South, viewed from a philosophic distance), and she was anxious to tell me how she had written it:

"For many years I had been thinking about it and finally wrote it this past year. One page a day is all I could do, typing with one hand [she did not have the use of her left hand]. And even that I owe to my doctor, Mary Mercer, to whom I dedicated my book. For years after the strokes [there were three after she was twenty-nine], I had a block about writing. The doctors gave me up, see. . . . Then I found Mary. I went to her one day and said, 'Darling, I've lost my soul!' 'No, you haven't,' she said. It was a sublime experience, what she did for me. Many days I would write in her home. We became good friends."

She spoke blandly, without emotion, pausing only to pick up her drink and start a cigarette.

Most of her writing on the book had been done on a large marble-top table in an adjoining room which overlooked the garden and the Hudson River. The beautiful slab of stone was one of her prized possessions, she said, bought with the money she had made on the movie of her novel, *Member of the Wedding.* She recalled how Ida had wept inconsolably when recently the marble had cracked under the weight of books. "Well, I nearly cried too, but I told Ida, 'It's only material, darling, and material things outlive us!' "

The story reminded her of other things of beauty she had acquired over the years: an antique gold statue she had bought for a song in a little French village, an exquisite Persian rug a vendor had brought to her door in Italy, and her delicate white organdy curtains, a recent "special purchase."

When the talk turned from decorating, invaluable Ida and other people she loved (Tennessee Williams, "Winston" Auden, Gypsy Rose Lee and Henry Varnum Poor) to literary matters, Carson Mc-Cullers preferred to listen. Beyond the admission that she had always worked hard at her writing, and naming, when prodded, the writers she admired (Faulkner, Joyce, Dostoevsky, Tolstoy—the last two she read regularly, along with the *Ladies' Home Journal, McCall's,* and the *Daily News*), beyond such casual admissions, she shied from discussing literature or her own writing. She had once written: "Writing is a wandering, dreaming occupation." Remote from literary fashions ("Who is Jack Kerouac?" she asked), she had never learned to intellectualize her art.

Yet she reads the critics and takes them seriously. "They've made me weep! One called me a corrupter of youth. Imagine!" Amused now in retrospect, she picked up her drink and put an end to the subject.

Briefly, the South claims her attention. She had been watching the Freedom Riders on television and she was feeling optimistic. "I believe in humanity" is her simple, unguarded response to all that the recent turmoil implies. Though she left her native Columbus, Georgia, more than twenty-five years ago, when she came East to start a concert career, she has not severed her ties with the South. Almost annually she visits her former piano teacher and her teacher's husband. "They are the 'We' of me. It was out of my feeling for them that I wrote *Member of the Wedding.*"

More relaxed, she turned the talk to things of the heart: loyal friends, the pain of loss, music, and that most heartful of composers, Schubert. "I wore out a record of 'Winterreise' in one week. My friends thought I was morbid. Imagine!" She lighted another cigarette and swept the listener with a deep look into her orbit.

It had grown dark, and the fading light accentuated her wraithlike figure. We touched on her blighted concert career. No regrets. Did she believe in fate? Carson McCullers's eyes grew wide; then, in a tone of confession:

"Not Fate. I believe in Grace. Not just God . . . do you know what I mean? Grace comes if you really try, if you believe in something—in people, in the soul. Then something you want happens. I guess it's God mainly. And it is also Love."

1961

It was these words, along with the general impact of that meeting in 1961, that led me back to Mrs. McCullers's writings and helped me see a dimension of her work I had virtually missed. Like most readers, I had recognized the mythic, "gothic" quality of her prose and had been stunned by the harsh, often morbid truths it imparted. Like most, too, I had been distracted by the phantasmagoria of despair and decay that overlay such works as *Reflections in a Golden Eye* (1941) and *The Ballad of the Sad Café* (1951).

Only a close reading of her work as a whole could reveal the muted, poetic apprehension that was the other side of the coin. Though more grotesque and violent in effect than a Flaubert or Mauriac when writing of the illogic of love, Mrs. McCullers could still be sophisticated in de-romanticizing the sentimental life. Without so much as a nod at explicit sex, she could chart the mutilation of hearts, the terrors of betrayed illusions. At the same time, with her balladlike stance (all behavior exaggerated or simplified in the interest of emotional truth) she could counter the ironic intent of her tales with an almost Tolstoyan affirmation of the human essence.

"Grace and love"—the equation had been made early in her career. This is one of the interesting revelations of the miscellany that Margarita G. Smith has pulled together from her sister's papers. This uneven collection of previously uncollected pieces titled *The Mortgaged Heart* includes ten apprentice stories (some with their teacher's comments attached), a few later stories, short essays and poems (some of them published in fashion magazines), the outline of her first novel,

The Heart Is a Lonely Hunter (published in 1940 when she was twenty-two), and, not least of all, a touching portrait of the author by her sister that rightly emphasizes "the moments of joy" rather than of pain. The volume's most obvious usefulness will be to students of literature who will be able to scan her early work for essential patterns and learn the extent to which personal experiences shaped her art.

At seventeen, in a story titled "Sucker," she could already distinguish between two forms of love: the delusive, romantic love, doomed by its nature to disappointment and pain, and a gratuitously given fraternal love that knows no distinction of age, sex or rank. The elder of two adolescent brothers, having cruelly rebuffed the younger, who worships him, and having in turn been rejected by his girl, muses: "There is one thing I've learned. If a person admires you a lot, you despise him and don't care—it is the person who doesn't notice you that you are apt to admire."

This perversity of passionate love would later be made palpable and awesome by Mrs. McCullers's weird choice of lovers—among them a deaf-mute, a homosexual dwarf, and a twelve-year-old girl who falls in love with her brother's "wedding." All demonstrate what she formulates into a more extended theory of love that says, in sum: "Love is a solitary thing."

The idea itself is not original. It is the very stuff of romantic comedy, of comedy of manners. It is, most illustriously, Proust. What enabled Mrs. McCullers to make it her own was her lifting of it to a spiritual plane where a metamorphosis from a lower to a higher form of love could be envisaged if not always achieved. Miss Smith reports that as a youngster the author would practice Bach fugues for five hours a day. She was never to become a concert pianist, but the special discipline of music must have been behind the ease with which she learned to capture her characters at moments of highest emotional pitch, making meaning conspire with mood. In an early story, "Court in the West Eighties," a young girl fantasizing about her neighbors, whom she glimpses from her court window, reveals in the process her own suppressed sense of isolation. In microcosm, it is the same anxiety that prompts the anguished nightmares and hallucinations of *Reflections in a Golden Eye.*

The literary style of the late 1930s and 1940s was largely naturalistic, and it is not surprising to find Mrs. McCullers straining to meet its demands (her teacher is always warning her against becoming too "inward"). It accounts for the woman's magazine slickness of some of her later stories and also, I think, the slightly cloying wistfulness of *Member of the Wedding.* Yet in one respect naturalism gave her an important cue, as it did the early Saroyan and Nathanael West: through her awareness of the social crisis of the period—the Depression—she was able to give edge to her theme of spiritual isolation. The two central figures of *The Heart Is a Lonely Hunter* (titled *The Mutes* in her outline), the deaf-mutes, Singer and Antonapoulos, may be seen as embodiments of a general atrophy of communication in "a wasteful, shortsighted society" where people are forced into work that denies their "deepest nature." The love that exists between these two, as between the other frustrated or disadvantaged "couples" who share some inner truth, becomes a form of liberation from the social straitjacket.

This kind of perfect communion is not so easily visible in the novels of the next decade—a period so personally anguished for the author. In *Reflections,* the only lyric motif she sounds is in the tender fantasy of love between a woman on the verge of madness and her aesthetic Filipino houseboy. In *Member of the Wedding,* the kinship that exists between twelve-year-old Frankie, her six-year-old cousin, and a wise, talkative black cook is dissipated when Frankie enters stereotyped womanhood. Just as short-lived is the transformation that takes place in Miss Amelia when she falls in love with her misshapen cousin Lymon in *The Ballad.* Only in her last novel, a Faulknerian fable of racial turmoil in the South, does she allow a final triumph for "grace and love." In a luminous moment of love's metamorphosis, her hero discovers, as he looks down from his plane, that "the whole earth from a great distance means less than a pair of human eyes.

Even the eyes of the enemy." Toward the end of her life, as at the beginning, Mrs. McCullers was clutching at the prospect of human liberation through a new contagion of love.

1972

Affirmation and Love in T. S. Eliot

It is my experience," remarked T. S. Eliot in his 1940 lecture on Yeats, "that toward middle age a man has three choices: to stop writing altogether, to repeat himself . . . or . . . to adapt himself to middle age and find a different way of working."

The different way of working for Eliot in his middle years was the theater. Except for *Sweeney Agonistes* (1926-27), an experiment in "Aristophanic melodrama," all his dramatic writing was done after his forty-fifth year, long after he had established his preeminence as the distinct poetic voice of the age.

The transition from solitary study to theatrical limelight is not an easy one to make at any age, and even for a poet practiced in the art of writing interior dramas (i.e., *The Love Song of J. Alfred Prufrock, Portrait of a Lady, The Waste Land,* etc.), the risks were great. But when, in 1933, Eliot undertook to collaborate on a religious pageant,

The Rock, with E. Martin Browne, the director of religious drama at the diocese in Chichester, he faced up to more than one challenge: he not only apprenticed himself to a demanding new medium—the theater—but also envisioned the possibility of bringing to it a new concept of poetic drama.

Ten years after the end of Eliot's playwriting career, Mr. Browne, who went on to produce all six of Eliot's plays (and who was also a close friend), tells in *The Making of T. S. Eliot's Plays* how that amalgam of poet and playwright evolved, and the part that he himself played in it. By reproducing early notations and manuscripts of the plays in various stages of composition (some of them not yet available to scholars), he is able to trace both Eliot's progress in stagecraft and the continuous course his experiments in the theater took. Far from minimizing the poet's genius, Mr. Browne's sometimes rambling but generally vivid book succeeds in enlarging our appreciation of Eliot's creative process, his extraordinary capacity to integrate past and present experiences.

A convert, in the nineteen-twenties, to Anglo-Catholicism, Eliot was drawn to Mr. Browne's scenario dealing with the building of a church in London. But mainly he welcomed the opportunity to try out an aspect of his theory of poetic drama. Dispensing with traditional blank verse, he modeled his Chorus on the liturgical form and transformed it by applying a coating of music hall, ballet and mime. If there were signs of the novice in *The Rock,* they were well hidden in the stunning production it received at Sadler's Wells.

Two years later, in *Murder in the Cathedral* (a title supplied by Mrs. Browne), Eliot sought a more important breakthrough to write verse that would intensify, not interrupt, the play's action. Writing for the Canterbury Festival, he utilized a historical subject—the martyrdom of Thomas à Becket—for his own ends.

Becket interested him at least as much psychologically as historically, and, because Eliot's religious and psychological insights converged, Becket as both man and saint became believable. But the play's staging problems were enormous, and only Mr. Browne's professional help finally assured its success.

In terms of his dramatic progress, Eliot saw the play (generally acclaimed "a masterpiece") as a mere "dead end." It was in his next dramatic venture, *The Family Reunion* (1937), that he would attempt to combine his artistic and philosophical faiths. By placing his poetry "on a thin diet" throughout most of the play, he hoped to reach greater intensity in its moments of illumination. And, in fact, he did. What bedeviled him in this play was the melodramatic plot: to expose the spiritual crisis of an unexceptional hero, he had transported the classical Eumenides to a conventional upper-middle-class drawing room. Though aware of the many problems he had unleashed, he resisted Mr. Browne's advice for the first time, complaining: "Some of your criticisms seem to me tantamount to asking me to write a new play."

By the middle of the book, Mr. Browne appears, indeed, to have lost touch with Eliot's evolving experiments, even seems to miss the point. He is uneasy with the playwright's foray into comedy in *The Cocktail Party* (1947) and *The Confidential Clerk* (1953)—particularly with the extreme form that Eliotic reconciliation takes in them. Nor is it simply that the sophisticated and fashionable settings of those plays jar with the quest for spiritual dimension. More seriously, Mr. Browne concludes: "Eliot placed upon his genius a regrettable limitation. He tied himself to social, and still more to theatrical, conventions which were already outworn when the plays were written."

Perhaps. But Eliot could not be deflected from his course. His final play, *The Elder Statesman,* written at the age of seventy, was nearly stripped of "poetry" on the theory that the play's very essence was poetic. It was Eliot's last stab at making poetry of "natural utterance."

Written in 1958, a year after Eliot's marriage to Valerie Fletcher, *The Elder Statesman* derives unmistakably from the Eliot of the early and middle years. The "different ways of working" in middle age also involved "experiencing new emotions appropriate to one's age," Eliot thought. "The new emotion" he experienced—love, earthly love—appropriate at any age, was particularly right for him in the light of his happy marriage. It can be no mere coincidence that this most serene work of the elder poet was dedicated to his wife, "To whom I owe the leaping delight/That quickens my senses in our wakingtime."

Indeed, Eliot confessed now to a new hopefulness and calm. To his erstwhile defeatist question, "Why should the agèd eagle stretch his wings?" he found it possible in *The Elder Statesman* to offer as positive an answer as he has dared to give—and this time in secular terms, which should pose no difficulties to modern audiences. In the reading, it seems the inevitable coda to the evolving Divine Comedy of modern life which Eliot's work as a whole suggests.

Eliot's plays, all written since his conversion to Anglicanism in the late twenties, have depicted life as a delusive ritual of appearances in which the essential struggle is the liberation of the authentic self. Because his religious and psychological insights have converged, his meaning, even in such obviously religious plays as *Murder in the Cathedral*, has never been simply doctrinaire. By identifying the religious concepts of contrition and purgation with the psychoanalytical process involving the social Persona and the real Self that lies below it, he discovered a new moral approach to character.

What has distinguished his heroes in the past has been their capacity and willingness to suffer in the hope of finding the elusive meaning of their existence. Stripped of their masks, and vulnerable before their fate, they have accepted the ultimate consequence: renunciation of their social being and ordinary human relationships. To suggest their susceptibility to intangible truths, Eliot has not hesitated to use unrealistic devices such as Tempters, ghosts and divine confessors in disguise. Mainly through the mystical overtones of his poetry, he has persuaded us that these are of another order of human beings.

The fact that *The Elder Statesman* is bare of such devices indicates that the demand on the hero has greatly lessened. In Lord Claverton, the central character, the play has a considerably modified Eliot hero: An aging public figure, condemned by ill health to retire, Claverton has only a brief stop to make in his "purgatory" before he is released from the burden of his "guilt." In a lifetime of riding on the high tide of success, he has never been troubled by his conscience, and it is only awakened on the eve of his retirement when by accident he meets two figures from his remote past who remind him of moral failures in his youth. One, a former Oxford classmate now turned into a cynical Central American businessman, draws a likely parallel between his own fraudulent life and the statesman's; the other, an aging musical comedy star, recalling how he had callously jilted her, pricks his ego by observing:

> *The difference between an elder statesman*
> *And posing successfully as an elder statesman*
> *Is practically negligible. And you look the part.*

But Claverton does not sense his counterfeit image until he is also confronted by his son, Michael, who protests that as the son of a famous father he has been denied the right of realizing himself. In the midst of advising Michael not to run away from his past failures, Claverton has a sudden illumination about himself, and, growing humble, he asks:

> *Do I understand the meaning*
> *Of the lesson I would teach?*

Turning to his daughter, Monica, he adds: *Is it too late for me?*

Apparently it is not too late. For in the next act, having confessed all his transgressions to Monica, Claverton has the courage and insight to acknowledge himself *"a broken-down actor"* who has never loved anyone. Yes, he has loved Monica, *but there's the impediment./It is impossible to be quite honest with your child.*

> *How could I be sure that she would love the actor*
> *If she saw him, off-stage, without*
> *His costume and his make-up?*

Nor could he turn to his wife while she lived:

> *How open one's heart*
> *When one is sure of the wrong response?*

Only in the realization of Monica's steadfast love can he finally accept himself. There is potential pathos in his lines:

> *If a man has one person, just one in his life*
> *To whom he is willing to confess everything . . .*
> *Then he loves that person, and his love will save him—*

In this concept of love as a catalyst in self-realization, Eliot has come a long way from *The Cocktail Party,* where one encountered at every turn the counterfeit faces which lovers create to meet their own needs.

Although the religious implication in this new insight is muted, the play unmistakably suggests the "Paradiso" episode of the poet's Divine Comedy. For here, without strife or suffering, and in the presence of a loving, forgiving person, the penitent finds both freedom and bliss.

It is, perhaps, in the nature of a "Paradiso" to lack drama. But what adds to the static quality of the play is a central character who is too abstractly conceived to be anything more than a mouthpiece for the poet. And in the absence of his "special language," Eliot's leaning toward Victorian plotting is unhappily emphasized. But as philosophy it marks a turning-point. From the questioning which began with *Ash Wednesday,* Eliot has moved on to an affirmation which is essentially Dantesque.

1959

Huxley Revisited

The literary critics have not yet gone to work on Aldous Huxley—though he has been dead now for several years. His death of cancer at sixty-nine on the day President Kennedy was assassinated nearly caught the press off its guard. When the tributes finally came, they centered on the man rather than on his art. The popular image so far projected of him, as a satirist or Utopian, does him an injustice: it fails to encompass the scope of his gifts or account for the paradoxes of his thought. The witty, sardonic novelist of the twenties and early thirties, the formidably learned essayist and sensitive art critic, the prophetic social thinker and the quasi-mystic who envisioned a regenerated Brave New World—all are strands of a complex of achievements that will have to be sorted before his true stature can be known.

The nearly simultaneous publication of three books on Huxley suggests that a reconstruction of the British writer's personal image, at least, is at hand. Ronald Clark's multibiography of the Huxley clan, *The Huxleys,* and a revised edition of a 1957 study by John Atkins document the life and works. And in *This Timeless Moment* Laura Huxley, Huxley's second wife, reviews the last fifteen years of his life, when both his fiction and his personality increasingly testified to his involvement with mystical Eastern religions and his experiments with psychedelic drugs. Despite its soap-opera title and occasional discursiveness, Mrs. Huxley's memoir makes absorbing reading. It captures, if not the totality of Huxley's genius, certain integral and warmly human aspects of it.

When in 1948 Laura Achera first met Aldous and Maria Huxley in their home near Los Angeles, the fifty-four-year-old author was still a strikingly handsome, slightly willowy figure, a bit remote with strangers (because of his impaired eyesight) but thoroughly alive, with a virile energy and charm that had nothing in them of the mystic. Though he had not yet made his pioneering experiments with mescaline or other hallucinogenic drugs (he was to help coin the word "psychedelic" in 1957), he was absorbed in the study of mind expansion as practiced by the mystics. And, while he had not abandoned his physiological interest in man, two recent works, *Time Must Have a Stop* and *The Perennial Philosophy,* had left no doubt that he had moved radically away from rigidly rational and abstract thought.

Laura, a former concert violinist turned film editor and amateur psychotherapist (twenty years his junior), had no intellectual pretensions, but she had what Huxley must have regarded as a greater gift: a lively perceptiveness and—one might add, having read this book—a Lawrentian heroine's openness to experience.

At the suggestion of Huxley's wife, Laura and Aldous became collaborators in therapeutic sessions that ten years later would be incorporated into his last novel, *Island.* Laura's friendship with "two marvelous human beings" continued until Maria died in 1955; a year later she was married to Huxley.

Writing impressionistically, Mrs. Huxley often breaks the thread of her narrative with suggestive "asides": a sheaf of Huxley's personal letters, key passages in his work (including the first chapter of an unfinished last novel), and flashbacks to some peripheral event. Always she is careful to trace the lines that will fix the true man. She is endlessly impressed with his gentleness, his goodwill and the boldness of his imagination. And she is aware of his many-sidedness. Their "secret" instant wedding at a drive-in chapel in Yuma has the extravagant romantic humor of a Cary Grant movie, and at the same time a sober overtone. Breaking the news of his marriage to his son, he writes: "Tenderness is the best memorial to tenderness."

Mrs. Huxley's close identification with her husband's private world is made evident in her sympathetic but unsentimental appraisal of his lifelong battle with failing eyesight and her recognition of his unobtrusive heroism in the face of his serious illness and his increasingly daring spiritual quests. When a cruel brush fire destroys their home and his books and manuscripts in 1961, she reports not only his stoic response but the dry humor with which he accepted the event as "a hint from the higher power that books weren't the solution to the problems of life." And when, after one of his psychedelic sessions, he remarks: "I want to know and constantly be in a state of love," she writes: "I wondered. To me Aldous seemed always to be in a state of love."

That love had its sensual as well as spiritual meaning. "Can I ever complete you as you complete me?" he asks Laura in a letter that belies the myth of his cold intellectuality. The nature and extent of her own devotion to him is revealed in her restrained account of the final week of his life when she was torn between saving him from the knowledge of his impending death and helping him to die the conscious death he desired. When, at the end of a painful dictation of his last essay, he asked her for a dose of LSD, she knew that he was ready for that final adventure.

Huxley's quest, as his wife is at pains to point out, had not stopped at personal salvation. Even his most extreme work, *The Doors of Perception,* contained warnings against addiction to an "ecstatic consciousness" that would cut off the individual from the rest of the world. "Will you merely enjoy them [the psychedelic 'trips'] as you would enjoy an evening at the puppet show and then go back to business as usual?" asks the doctor in his Utopian novel *Island.* The tone of misgiving clearly belongs to Huxley, whose mysticism, to the end, had a strong social basis.

1968

Shaw and His Boswell

Archibald Henderson's biography, *George Bernard Shaw: Man of the Century,* is a labor of love. Encyclopedic in size and scope, it makes Boswell's *Life of Johnson* seem a relatively simple endeavor. For while Johnson was a man of many parts, Shaw, who outlived him by nineteen years, was a veritable anthology. Nor was this opinionated dramatist, philosopher and socialist content to sit back and hold court in some tavern or club; "man of the century" that he was, he came by his opinions the hard way, through firsthand experience in the mêlée of public life. Indeed, for Shaw, literature came as a result of life, not as an excuse for it.

But if the figure of Shaw looms larger by far than Johnson's, that of Henderson, his prolific biographer, suffers by comparison with the irresistible little Scotsman. Meeting Shaw in 1907 when the playwright (like Johnson when Boswell first met him) was just past his fiftieth birthday, Henderson brought to his task as official biographer much the same worshipful enthusiasm and persistence and a fair measure of personal charm. Though lacking in Boswell's provocative ingenuousness (the interviewer's happiest gift), Henderson brought, to his own credit, the training of a scholar and an informed concern with human welfare that was a fair match to Shaw's own. His many books about Shaw have played so large a part in forming our image of the playwright that we are hard put to evaluate his work. It is only when we consider the present volume in relation to other monumental biographies that certain chinks in Henderson's armor begin to show.

As Shaw's plays grow increasingly popular in performance, what we find wanting in a standard reference work such as Henderson's is the feel of the man behind the prototype. Now that all the wonderful tales about Shaw have been told and all his *bons mots* recorded, we are ready to have his views explored as well as explained. In his role as a critic of Shaw, Henderson was in a sense too close to the man, too enmeshed in his day-to-day life to achieve complete perspective. As a biographer, he was neither close enough in the obtrusive manner of a Boswell nor detached enough to fully succeed in translating the myth into the man. To get close to genius takes a kind of genius, too, one suspects. But a pitfall for the biographer may also lie in the subject's resistance to being humanized.

Shaw from the first gave Henderson fair warning of the kind of biography he expected of him. He wrote: "A thorough biography of any man who is up to his chin in the life of his own time as I have been is worth writing about as an *historical* document. . . . Make me a peg on which to hang a study of the last half of the nineteenth century. I am treating you as a possible Gibbon. I urge you to treat yourself so."

Taking Shaw's order to heart, Henderson emphasized the political man in Shaw and stumbled on an important new dimension in biographical writing. But while historically his portrait is vivid and true, humanly it tends to blur, with no doors opening on that inner core of being where all contradictory impulses and actions are resolved.

Several times in the early part of the narrative, Henderson appears to be on the verge of revelation. He indicates conflicts in Shaw which stemmed from childhood years spent amid genteel poverty in a loveless household. But instead of analyzing these conflicts in terms of Shaw's character as a whole, he prefers to explain them away one by one. When he finds a human failing in Shaw, his first impulse is to rationalize it. Thus he brands Shaw's habit of ridiculing members of his family as "unhuman" but justifies it on the ground that they made perfect subjects of satiric distortion.

But there is a larger obstacle in Henderson's path, one with which Boswell never had to contend. When Johnson stated an opinion, he meant every word in its literal sense; all Boswell had to do was to report it word for word. With Shaw it is quite a different matter. His subtle mind, his satirical, quixotic manner of expression are in constant need of interpretation. (Shaw, knowing this, gives it to us himself in his prefaces—but again it's Shaw-style.) In his determination to note everything of consequence that Shaw ever uttered or committed to writing, Henderson too often finds himself short of space for comment or interpretation. At times the omission is quite startling, as when, following a revealing quotation in which Shaw recalls being antagonized as a child by his father's unrealistic snobbishness, he suggests no reaction, turning quickly to something else.

In his portraiture of Shaw the Socialist, however, he is far less shy of comment. Here he is on secure ground. Believing that "Shaw is essentially an economist," he devotes more than two hundred pages to the playwright's activities as a Fabian. Beginning with Shaw's early days in the movement, when he was still a struggling novelist serving his apprenticeship as a critic of music, art and drama, Henderson traces "the metamorphosis of a shy, reflective dreamer into a challenging fighter." His impassioned response to Henry George and *Das Kapital,* his association with the intellectually congenial Webbs left their indelible mark. On the one hand, he wrote a Marxist novel, *The Unsocial Socialist,* and, on the other, he was launched on a new vocation—propaganda lecturing and writing.

To this "revolted *bourgeois,*" as Henderson aptly calls him, the experience of lecturing was totally exhilarating. "Every Sunday," Shaw boasted, "I lectured on a subject I wanted to teach myself." But because he gave himself no proletarian airs, was vituperative without being common and instructive without being dull, he soon gained a reputation as a "mischief-maker and privileged lunatic."

Literal-minded Socialists like H. G. Wells did not appreciate Shaw's brand of irreverent humor, which spared no one, not even the Socialists. Indeed, the high intellectual level on which the Fabians operated under the influence of Shaw was chiefly responsible, Henderson points out, for the label they acquired as "armchair socialists and parlor performers."

After the success of the Russian Revolution, Shaw, like the Webbs, abandoned the doctrine of the "inevitability of gradualness," but, unlike the Webbs, who embraced Sovietism, he remained ambiguous and inconsistent in his attitude toward Russia. He accepted the Revolution as a fact and saw in it a great victory for Socialism. But though he talked like a convert after his visit to Russia in 1931, his motives were often mixed. Henderson aptly quotes Sir Osmond Ovey, the British Ambassador, who observed:

"Of course the Russians don't realize that Shaw is an Irishman, which naturally means anti-British and unrepresentative. He has been growing more and more Irish every day since he has been in Moscow."

For the first time, Henderson's faith in Shaw's Socratic wisdom appears weakened. And on the face of it understandably so. For there is much in his pronouncements and in such plays as *Geneva* and *On the Rocks* which smacks of the propagandist in a subversive cause. But there were factors influencing Shaw's attitude for which Henderson does not fully account, though they are implicit in his books— namely, Shaw's impressionableness to newness and change on the social scene, the delight he took in playing the devil's disciple, and the propensity he had for the Swiftian method of shocking men back to sanity. For its own good, he wanted democracy put on the spot.

Although Henderson is no longer in search of a systematic philosopher in Shaw, he still appears baffled by inconsistencies in his thinking. He might recall that the problem was brilliantly argued some time ago by Edmund Wilson, who observed that Shaw was first of all an artist who combined three different points of view that were inevitably in conflict—that of the practical man, of the socialist reorganizer of society, and of the poet-philosopher. If the artist in Shaw profited by his triple vision, the thinker in Shaw often lapsed into ambiguity and confusion because of it. Thus, for a synthesis of Shaw, nothing has yet replaced the record of the plays themselves.

As anyone who has ever attended a Shaw play knows, a great part of the fascination of his comic dramas derives from the fact that he will not let you believe too wholeheartedly and too long in anything at all, lest by so doing we create a new orthodoxy. His plays are a testimony of the falseness of modern man's ideals, of his mistaken notions of heroism, history, science, love—of truth itself. His own single constant faith, his obsession with the cult of the superior person, led him temporarily to a false ideal; favoring a strong hand in government, he all but exalted dictatorship.

Was Shaw the anti-environmentalist, the believer in the Life Force and the exceptional person, truly a "man of the century," or was he the prophet of a new dawn in which individualism and social responsibility would no longer cancel each other out? Henderson has set the stage. It remains for future biographers to search the drama that was Shaw himself.

1957

Memo: To Bernard Shaw

I am writing this review of the second volume of your *Collected Letters, 1898-1910,* edited by Dan H. Laurence, in the form of a memo because I would like to keep my comments and criticisms strictly between ourselves. Ever since my teens, when I saw my first Shaw play, I have been a hopeless Shavian, and I can't help wondering (a bit apprehensively) what effect this batch of letters from your middle years will have on your literary image. It is in the nature of personal letters to reveal chinks in the writer's armor—isn't that why we are tempted by other people's mail?—and yours add a dimension that remained obscure even to your Boswell, Archibald Henderson.

To be perfectly frank, Mr. Shaw, the fascination of your letters in this twelve-year period does not stem from the brilliance of mind and engaging wit for which you are rightly honored. Hastily written or drawn out to article length, they are not (thank God) to be read as models of epistolary art, but neither do they suggest, except vaguely, the quality of genius that went into the writing of *Major Barbara, Man and Superman* and *Candida* (to name only three plays of this period) or those mind-opening, playful *Prefaces.* Yet these meticulously (if a bit too succinctly) edited letters could be of absorbing interest to Shavians bored with the myth of the oracular sage. Even without the ardent letters to Mrs. Patrick Campbell, which belong in the next volume, we can see that you are not, after all, a historical document, but only a rather complicated man.

Consider the circumstances surrounding your marriage, at age forty-one, to the millionairess Charlotte Payne-Townshend. Was it mere coincidence that after your two decades of "philandering" in London, your resistance to marriage (an institution you didn't much approve of) failed you just as a series of minor accidents condemned you to long months of semi-invalidism? Coincidence, too, that the marriage came on the heels of your resignation from salaried journalism and the launching of a playwriting career whose financial rewards would long remain precarious? You give yourself away in a letter to Ellen Terry soon after your honeymoon in 1898: "Now that my health is returning, I love you as much as ever, in the ungentlemanliest and ungodliest manner."

That romance was only on paper—but how sensible of you to keep it so. Life with a celebrated actress could never have provided the stability you needed to produce one masterpiece after another, while at the same time you actively engaged in local politics, propagandized Fabian Socialism, found and rehearsed your leading ladies, and frantically scribbled away all those articles, lectures and letters. You might at least have acknowledged your blessing; instead you are forever succumbing to the adulations of young adoring ladies. Poor Charlotte.

Your forte, obviously, was not in personal relationships, though in Charlotte's words (spoken bitterly?) you were "quite friendly and sympathetic with everybody, from dogs and cats to dukes and duchesses." But, oh, that headmaster complex! No real exchange of ideas—only the need to drive sense into your "charges." In the strident tone of Councilman Shaw promoting Free Trade or attacking play censorship, you must have the last word, whether you are dealing with a stranger (Laurence Irving: "You were a volcano smouldering with unuttered wrongs from your first step on stage . . ."), a critic friend (William Archer: "You are a sort of child in fairyland who has never learned to live in the world . . ."), or your "ruffian" publisher, Grant Richards.

Memo: To Bernard Shaw

A master at ferreting man's delusions, you give specious, patronizing advice to your translator, S. Trebitsch: "You should give up literature and take to politics. I owe all my originality, such as it is, to my determination not to be a literary man. Instead of drinking and discussing authors and reviews, I sit on committees with practical greengrocers and bootmakers. . . . You must do the same. Keep away from books and from men who get their ideas from books."

The year is 1902, and you have already written five novels and ten plays for the Theater of Ideas, published studies of Ibsen and Wagner, and edited the Fabian Essays. Plus, you have gobbled up Henry George, Marx and Nietzsche. Stay away from books, indeed!

Not that we question your sense of involvement as you urge H. G. Wells to "learn the habits of the political human animal as the naturalist learns the habits of the wasps by watching them," but we would rather you told us what you observed instead of ranting on about being a Socialist, an anti-individualist, anti this, anti that. If one did not know your plays with their essential sanity, their paradoxical mixture of rebellion and reasonableness, one might take you for some kind of dabbler in the New Politics, showing off the brilliance of your Irish mind. In the absence of your humor, the elixir of your art, the gap between what you say and what you do looms large.

With all your "committee habit," you are not convincing in the role of anti-Establishment rebel. A keen businessman, you are forever badgering your publisher, who ends up bankrupt; despite your cavalier suggestion to Wells that the four of you try "group marriage," you remain morally above reproach; and always you have the Victorian's compulsion for work. Though hard to admit, your harangues against Rationalism, Determinism, Materialism, etc. sound appallingly banal when detached from the vitality of your stage creations. All too rare in this volume are glimpses of that other Shaw, the dramatist of vision. Writing to Henry James, you sum up the real source of your power in the theater:

"I, as a Socialist, have had to preach . . . the enormous power of the environment. But I never idolized environment as a dead destiny.

We can change it: we must change it: there is absolutely no other sense in life than the work of changing it."

Reading that, I wonder if you are not bored out there in the Beyond, where all "change" has ceased, and perhaps making plans for reincarnation. What a field day you would have here just now with your canny insights into the "political human animal." And you would give our theater, so threadbare of intellectual tension, a shot in the arm. We cannot promise you instant success, nor even another Charlotte. But there would be no dearth of adoring Shavians, among them

Yours ever faithfully, if critically,

N. B.

1972

Reviews by Trilling

As a critic, Lionel Trilling occupies a unique position in American letters. It is his name which comes first to mind when we wish to soften the charges against the New Criticism, his name again we cite when we want to argue for the humanistic discipline. Indeed he is one of the few serious critics of our day who can write at the same time for the *Partisan Review,* the *New Yorker,* the *Nation,* the *New York Times,* the *New Leader* and any number of academic journals—not to mention the monthly bulletin of a well-known book club where many of the eminently readable essays in *A Gathering of Fugitives* originally appeared.

The fact that Mr. Trilling can maintain such a broad base of operation does not mean that he is eclectic; his style and approach never really vary. It means, rather, that his literary interests are part of a larger critical concern, to discover and define the meaning of our time. Yet this curiosity has little in common with the anthropological and sociological searches into our mores which make us feel "dead" before we know we are alive. There is in his relationship to the present something of the attitude of the artist who (in his own words) "is consumed by the desire to know how things are, who has entered into an elaborate romance with reality."

It is this unrelenting pursuit of "how things really are" that lends compelling interest to even the most casual literary commentary in this miscellaneous collection of reviews and articles on a variety of authors—among them two nonliterary figures, Freud and David Riesman. Whether he is taking a fresh look at the literature of another day, reviewing a current novel, or analyzing the "intangible" aspects of culture, he is careful to check traditional values and stock responses against his own experience of reality. Thus his viewpoints are often delightfully unexpected, with flashes of insight that bring us into a new relationship with writers of the past.

In one essay, for instance, we are introduced to a "modern" Dickens whom even the most sophisticated reader could appreciate. With the stigma of sentimentality removed, Dickens stands revealed as a precursor of Kafka, Proust and Joyce in his treatment of family relations. In the same way, he liberates Zola from the curse of naturalism when he writes about him: "The obsessive contemplation of the objectivity of objects, the thingness of things, is a step toward surrealism, perhaps toward madness." More interesting still is the angle from which he views that complex figure Henry Adams. Not the man himself, nor simply his work, but the attitude of ambivalence he inspires in the modern reader is what Mr. Trilling finds important to discuss, for he sees in ambivalence "an element of our thought and instrument of our intelligence." By involving ourselves even with what we do not especially admire, we are able to see things as they are, place values in their proper perspective.

Mr. Trilling's usefulness to the modern reader, we come to realize, consists as much in his sensitivity to and awareness of the life around him as in his aesthetic appreciation of literature. Modern fiction with its tendency to "render" rather than narrate must increasingly tax the reader's power of interpretation and make him dependent on the critic in a new way. From this standpoint, Mr. Trilling's critical impulse is consistently in the right direction. When, in one of the most original pieces in this volume, "The Morality of Inertia," Mr. Trilling points out why *Ethan Frome* does not qualify as a classic, we are as much interested in his conclusions about the morality he sees depicted in that novel as in his judgment of it as a work of art.

Examining the truthfulness of what the writer purports to say becomes an important part of the task of interpretation. In reviewing current fiction, Mr. Trilling's first concern is to discriminate between the sincere writer and the false one. If he can show that the novelist has presented an accurate picture of society or, in the larger sense, a particular culture, he is not troubled by his minor stature as an artist. So long as a C. P. Snow or a Robert Graves has "something to tell us," he is worthy of our close attention. By the same token, Mr. Trilling decries the work of a novelist like C. Virgil Gheorghiu because, despite its skill and persuasiveness, it falls short of the essential truth in its conclusions.

One cannot read Mr. Trilling's admirable essay "The Situation of the American Intellectual at the Present Time" (here expanded from its original form in the *Partisan Review*) without realizing how pertinent his conclusions are to the whole problem of modern literary criticism. Turning the tables on the intellectuals, he argues that it is not ideas that are lacking on the American cultural scene but *criticism* of ideas. This is lacking, he suggests, because the so-called intellectuals are unaware of influences coming from channels other than the limited literary field they know. Mr. Trilling's plea for greater critical interest in such fields as education, psychology, religion, and the other arts is in essence a plea for the expansion of the imagination and the capacity for integrated thought.

There is the ring of a critical manifesto in his concluding words: "Whatever the particular facts of our cultural situation may turn out to be, the recollection of Thoreau and Melville will sustain me in my certitude that the kind of critical interest I am asking the literary intellectual to take in the life around him is a proper interest of the literary mind, and that it is the right ground on which to approach transcendent things. . . . Art, strange and sad as it may be to have to say it again, really is the criticism of life."

When "the criticism of life" is more implicit than apparent, as in much of modern literature, we need more than ever critics who combine sensibility with a sense of fact. Mr. Trilling proves once again that the combination is possible.

1957

Criticism Par Excellence: V. S. Pritchett

I s this an age of criticism? The reputable critic who so generalized a while back was inviting trouble. The mock quality of his intent was invariably lost, and the phrase as literal truth is rapidly circulating. Yet, what could be more controversial? It would take a naïve optimist indeed to deny the paradox of our literary scene: that while more and more readers are taking their literary pleasures at second hand (via criticism), the real discipline of criticism is becoming more difficult than ever to achieve.

In our time, the critic's prestige has improved only because his *utilitarian* function has become more clearly defined. We turn to the critics more often to save ourselves time than to refine our enjoyment. In this scheme of things, Eliot's "perfect critic"—the free intelligence wholly devoted to inquiry—is the uneasy stranger, the marvelous exception.

In mid-century England, where the "impractical" man of letters is still an acceptable (if impoverished) figure, the situation has not come to quite this impasse. Yet, the English critic has his own battles to fight. Secure in a tradition dominated by personalities—from Hazlitt to Coleridge, to Arnold and Pater and Forster—he stands in danger of making his criticism too personal, his judgments too eccentric. His problem is to become broader, more catholic—and thereby more accessible—without losing his precious individuality. I know of few critics writing in the English language who strive so consistently to achieve this end as does V. S. Pritchett, whose *Books in General* is an excellent case in point.

In his capacity as literary critic of the *New Statesman and Nation,* Pritchett, who is also an admirable novelist and short-story writer, has given the lie to the notion that reviewing is an inferior form of criticism. He has shown that, in fact, it makes greater demands on the critic as a responsive human being living in a society of mutual concerns. Breadth of sympathy and a truly free intelligence have been his guarantee against snap judgments; they have enabled him to see simultaneously the virtues of such opposite writers as Chekhov and de Maupassant, to admit the failings of a Faulkner while praising his qualities. He has proved, finally, that loose and careless writing need not mar a reviewer's work. For sheer excellence of style, for wealth of precisely felt observations, there is little to compare with the intrinsic reading pleasure of Pritchett's criticism.

Pleasure is indeed what Pritchett modestly claims as his aim in reading. He calls himself "the ordinary reader" intent on discovering "the new point in life" from which any important literary work begins. His previous collection of reviews, aptly titled *The Living Novel,* considered the classics with a freshness and originality that made each shine anew with life. As an "expectant novelist" (then), he showed that he valued the novel as a form and communicated his excitement at discovering the variety of effects it could achieve. What he sought to establish was not a final judgment of a classic—the principle of pleasure to which he subscribes would make that difficult, if not impossible—but a true basis of exchange between the world of a Fielding or a Balzac and the world of today. In the novelist's individual approach he saw the alchemy by which these two worlds were made to meet.

In *Books in General,* which includes criticism of more recent fiction as well as biography and travel, we are more than ever aware of the value Pritchett places on character as a point of departure. Yet, his is not the psychoanalytic interest of an Edmund Wilson. What Pritchett looks for in the character of a Carlyle, a Gide or a Poe is not simply the abnormality, but the particularity *transformed by art* which reveals itself as the essential quality of the work. When he speaks of Conrad in terms of "the sensibility of the émigré," when he shows that "the animal watchfulness of Maupassant is the watchfulness of a childhood not outgrown," or when he suggests that Poe's "terrors, his pains, his guilt, his punishment, his melancholy . . . are not presented as maladies to be cured and he does not wish to lose them," he is not only bringing new insights for the biographer but driving a wedge into a truer understanding of these writers' works.

Like every critic worth his salt, Pritchett has his predilections. He is particularly in his element when dealing with English comic writers from Sterne to Jacobs and Firbank—perhaps because the pleasure they provide him is mingled with social criticism of a sort he approves: the *humanistic* kind, whose target is whatever is mechanistic, false and anti-life in modern society. On the whole, he is much more in sympathy with the earthy values of the Italian and Spanish novelist (Verga and Galdos in particular) than with the sophistries of a Koestler or the soul-searchings of a James, a Gide. Yet, his evaluations of Koestler and Gide are among the most interesting, and his piece on James is at least just. Not using literature as a means to an end, he is not tempted to indulge his considerable persuasive powers at the expense of the truth.

1953

The Tragedy of Delusion: Criticism by Joyce Carol Oates

As a writer of fiction, Joyce Carol Oates has a bold and individual imagination. The apparent ease with which she turns out novels and stories (as well as poetry) is astounding in the light of her consistent skill and literary art. Beneath their relentlessly violent surfaces, her novels grope for transcendent meanings and, at their most ambitious, seek to locate the central mode or attitude of our time.

Now in *The Edge of Impossibility: Tragic Forms in Literature,* her first volume of critical writings, she demonstrates the same boldness and individuality in her reading of a literary genre that has undoubtedly influenced her work. Just as her fiction moves out of its social contours, so her criticism extends beyond its stated subject. The fact that she can see a common thread in the tragic vision of such diverse writers as Shakespeare, Thomas Mann, Ionesco, Melville, Yeats and Chekhov indicates the extent to which her imagination breaks through the barriers of literary genres, movements and periods. If we "rediscover" the novels, plays and poems she examines, it is not because of what she reveals about their inherent worth but because of the un-suspected meanings they assume within the broader concept of tragedy she proposes.

Countering George Steiner's verdict that the death of God means the death of tragedy, she asks for "a redefinition of God in terms of the furthest reaches of man's hallucination." Her "redefinition" in-volves her in an intricate spiral of philosophical speculations and poetic insights that directly hinge on our contemporary concern with the existential and the absurd, as well as with parody and metamor-phosis.

Undeniably, our understanding of tragedy has come a long way from Aristotle's definition and the forms of it that Shakespeare and the Romantic poets have made familiar. Fear and pity, expiation, catharsis, poetic justice assume a new complexion as the essential wor-thiness of man and the truths by which he lives are questioned. What never alters, in Miss Oates's view, is the self-destruction that lies at the root of tragedy, "the violent loss of self" that results from man's unending search for "the absolute dream."

Seeing a rational, existential ethic as the dominant vision of Shakespeare's *Troilus and Cressida,* she can cut through the play's sardonic satire to show us its most radical ironic aspect: the tragedy that lies in the impossibility of tragedy. "Where everything is seen in terms of merchandise, disease, food, cooking, and the glory of blood-shed," she concludes, "man's condition is never tragic." A similar refinement of tragedy reveals itself to her in the paradox at the core of Yeats's later plays; there, a poetic transcendence overcomes the anguished sense of mutability.

Between these two extremes of the non-tragic that spells tragedy to Miss Oates are more believable victims in the new mold. In her essay on Dostoevsky's *The Brothers Karamazov,* she argues convincingly for an existential interpretation of the tragic fate of Ivan as the perpetrator of an intellectual crime. His refusal to be avenged and to forgive are seen as signs not of the lapsed Christian but of the existen-tialist who, in assuming full responsibility for his actions, must suffer the bitter agony of the unatoned. In Melville's Pierre and Confidence Man, she finds an even greater negation of struggle. Unlike Captain Ahab, these heroes of the novelist's later work are limited in their capacity to suffer, but, as tragic victims of a "nihilism" that finds nothing and no one to avenge, they come closer even than Troilus to Miss Oates's definition of the "condition" of tragedy.

But nihilism also has its dynamic side when it involves the creative hero's Faustian will to transcend his human limitations. Skillfully weaving in and out of the heavy symbolism of Thomas Mann's last novel, *Doctor Faustus,* Miss Oates shows how the composer Adrian's tragedy is as irreversible in its existential form as the classic hero's— only the "gods" that seal his doom are within himself, self-created, and therefore immune to human error.

There is very little in Chekhov that on the face of it one can identify with the contemporary Ionesco, but in separate essays Miss Oates suggests that these two playwrights are linked by the concept of the absurd. Here she is dealing with the expression of the absurd through language and structure. Viewing Chekhov's plays as "tragedies of the impotence of will about to transform themselves into comedies because their characters are diminished human beings," she can see a parallel between the irrelevant talk their self-deception produces and the meaningless dialogues of Ionesco's bitter fantasies. She fails, however, to note a pathos in Chekhov that Ionesco cannot echo. No matter how much they are "diminished," Chekhov's characters retain traces of human dignity, while Ionesco's have been fixed into stereotypes. This makes for an important qualitative difference.

To believe in the possibility of tragedy based on total negation becomes no small feat when we are dealing with a writer whose power lies in abstraction. As her own analysis suggests, the tragedy of nihilism carried to its furthest point in the plays of Ionesco becomes a mere parody of itself. Where the ironic content so outweighs the pathetic and the disparity between what is desired and what is achieved is so slight, empathy evades us.

Elsewhere, in retrospect, the tragedy of delusion Miss Oates describes often seems to pertain more to the writer than to his literary creation. It is certainly conceivable that Yeats, Melville, Mann and Dostoevsky were putting their own quality of vision to test in these lesser, later works. Writing from a philosophical distance, they arouse fear and awe at the spectacle of life's absurdity, but only on an intellectual plane. Yet it goes without saying that to move us, tragedy must first of all involve the feelings.

1972

Poet of the Air— and Earth: Antoine de Saint-Exupéry

His name had an aristocratic ring. And perhaps better than anyone else he exemplified E. M. Forster's "aristocracy of the sensitive, the considerate and the plucky." A pioneer of the sky in the predawn of the space age, he breathed the romance of the air as no one had done before or has since. But in the brief span of his forty-four years, the adventures he most prized—and wanted to record—were those that had to do with the earth, with the world of men and their immutable link to each other. *Terre des Hommes* (*Man's Earth*) he titled the book that brought him international fame. Thirty years after its publication, *Wind, Sand and Stars* (as it was ineptly translated) survives as a model of poetic prose that extols without embarrassment man's "essence" as distinct from his "existence."

Antoine de Saint-Exupéry, living, writing and dying as no French author had done before him (he disappeared somewhere between Corsica and the Alps on a reconnaissance flight in the summer of 1944), was inevitably mythologized as a heroic figure in France's time of defeat, as well as denigrated, by a post-Sartrian generation, for his quasi-mystical idealism. In his compelling, definitive biography, *Antoine de Saint-Exupéry: His Life and Time,* Curtis Cate, who has lived and worked in France, fills out what has been written largely through the testimony of those who knew the writer at different stages of his life.

It is a huge book whose scope is larger than its biographical subject—and rightly so, since Saint-Exupéry's life touched the life of his country at so many significant points. At the same time, it does not slight the smaller human aspects of a very much earthborn "Saint-Ex": the comrade of the luminous smile, the bearlike feet, the puckish profile who loved to entertain with card tricks and comic drawings, who kept his hands busy devising mechanical gadgets while his mind explored the meaning of everything he was experiencing.

Born with the century, into an old French family whose roots were in Toulouse and Aix, Saint-Exupéry had an idyllic childhood, despite the loss of his father when he was only four. With a beautiful artistic mother to inspire him and a houseful of sisters and brothers responding to his literary gifts, Saint-Ex stored a rich reserve of inner stability on which to draw in his hazardous future career.

At the Jesuit Collège de Sainte Croix at Le Mans, and later at Ecole Bossuet, an orthodox Roman Catholic education failed to curb his "perennial adolescence." A child of the era, he supplemented moralistic reflections (Pascal and Nietzsche were favorite authors) with a very tangible interest in the flying machine—that magnificent new invention that had so recently been released from the fantasy world of Jules Verne—right there in Le Mans!

Inevitably, when Saint-Exupery's term of compulsory military service came up in 1921, he found himself in the newly formed, glamorous French Air Force. Thereafter, his experiences in the air, first as an apprentice flyer in Morocco, later as commercial air-mail pilot and flight record breaker, set a pattern that would be endlessly repeated, wherever he was flying. There was the struggle with inadequate machinery and radio communications, second only to struggle with the elements; the undemanding yet fiercely loyal friendships with pilots and machinists; the long stretches of solitude; and over all, the sense of being "plunged into the heart of the mystery." By separating him intermittently from the earth, flying helped preserve his perspective and fight the particularism that made men "mistake the stones for the cathedral."

Mr. Cate's greatest challenge comes in suggesting the quality of Saint-Exupéry's poetic vision. To lift quotes from the adventure books is to miss what is characteristic and original in Saint-Ex: the tersely expressed revelation coming after a long period of stress—in the desert, on the Andes, or, as in that paean to man's spirit, *Flight to Arras,* in a village doomed to destruction.

Mr. Cate is on surer ground when he is dealing with the aviator's social existence: Saint-Ex in the cafés of St. Germain des Prés, with his petite South American wife (the marriage is only briefly sketched), or with André Gide and the American expatriates, who helped him to get published. Saint-Ex, on the threshold of fame as author of a new kind of nonfiction novel, *South Mail* (1929) and *Night Flight* (1931), crossing the Atlantic to pioneer mail flights to Patagonia. Saint-Ex saving a friend's life on the icy peaks of the Andes and subsequently nearly drowning in the south of France.

As special correspondent for *Paris-Soir,* he visited the Soviet Union in 1935 and covered the Spanish Civil War in 1936. Evocative meditations on the human aspects of war and social upheaval, his dispatches contained impassioned pleas against the encroachment of totalitarianism in all its forms. Once so nonpolitical, Saint-Ex now turned *homme engagé.*

In a politically and morally confused France, Saint-Ex in 1940 . pleaded for unity and found his patriotism questioned. Alienated by the cowering Vichy régime on the one hand, and the sectarianism of de Gaulle's Free French on the other, he sought exile in New York. A best-selling author in America, he found, through articles and talks, a platform from which to argue for the United States' entry into the war. At the same time, he kept dejection at bay by writing an allegorical children's book, *The Little Prince,* and beginning a philosophical work he was never to finish, *Wisdom of the Sands.*

Barred by de Gaulle from flying in his own country, he rejoiced at the opportunity to serve from an American base in North Africa when this country entered the European war. Despite a badly bruised shoulder and advanced age, he was glad to be again a *participant,* after the unreality of French émigré life. The poet and the man of action remained inseparable to the end.

1970

Beautiful and Undammed: Stories by Fitzgerald

I n 1928, three years after *The Great Gatsby* had secured his literary reputation, F. Scott Fitzgerald turned to his early youth for the subject of a series of stories. In the ensuing four years, while he struggled to finish his new novel, *Tender Is the Night,* he published thirteen of them in *The Saturday Evening Post* to the tune of $3,500 and $4,000 each. Clearly, there was to be no "sequel" to *Gatsby*—the earnest nineteen thirties were encroaching on the wild nineteen twenties, with which his work had become identified—and, distracted by his own personal troubles, Fitzgerald was not rushing to cast his art into the new mold.

The longer the novel was delayed, the greater became the temptation to arrange these autobiographical stories into "a nice light novel." But while the idea appealed to both his editor and his agent, in the end the artist in Fitzgerald resisted such easy fame. Rather than force them into a synthetic novel, he published some of the best as part of a collection of his stories.

Fitzgerald was mainly right. Though they center on two main characters, *The Basil and Josephine Stories* lack dramatic progression, resembling in form those radio and TV serials about youth in its daily encounters with the facts of social life. But from this vantage point—and thanks to the editors' inspired idea of presenting them in sequence—we are able to sense another kind of progression: an unfolding design for his moral (but never crudely moralizing) themes and ideas. Here, as always, Fitzgerald sees in the interaction between character and society poetic truths that transcend sociology. Slight as they are they delight us, as fragments of a Mozart or Chopin do because we know the work as a whole.

Basil and his female counterpart, Josephine, are precocious, privileged children living in the Midwest just before World War I. *Enfants terribles* in their own way, they would never dream of rebelling by running away from school, like their latter-day version, Holden Caulfield. When Josephine at sixteen is expelled from school, she can count on her influential father to reinstate her. Both Basil (who has inherited wealth) and Josephine (who is Chicago Society) take their place in society for granted. What they are unsure of is the cornucopoia of values they face. Because their experience has kept pace with their understanding, they are not "outsiders" like Holden—what "phoniness" they detect is more in themselves than in others.

From age ten to seventeen, Basil's world is an amalgam of sports and girls—success in one signaling acceptance by his peers, in the other proving his personal worth. Josephine lives and breathes for the opposite sex, and, lucky for her, she is endowed with looks and charm. Idealized passion (never sex itself) is her passport to a life of thrills and glamour, and a calculating mind helps her "use" men toward that end. Yet she is no Becky Sharp. She is spirited youth raised to its highest pitch and made poignant by its inability to see beyond "the immediate, shimmering present."

Basil has the making of a Gatsby, that Jazz Age Quixote who (we see now) was Fitzgerald's alter ego. At age ten, in "That Kind of a Party," he is a sophisticated little bully, insolent and thoughtlessly cruel as he sets out to impress Dolly—or her "specter," since they haven't yet met. At fourteen, he fantasizes himself into the gentleman crook, Arsène Lupin, who gives him "a sense of extraordinary power

. . . untamed, demonic and free." One minute he schemes to destroy "pretty boy" Blair, the next he decides he likes him after all and would rather live "safely within the law."

Largely because he is unpopular at first in school, Basil falls captive to "the ecstasy of ambition." He vows to become "great and powerful." What he senses as his "unknown destiny" turns into the glamorous "mirage of Yale" and his dazzling future as a playwright. When a schoolmate converts him to "the perfect life," with moral responsibility for others, his "ecstasy" soars to new heights. But gab about it as he will, he is no catcher in the rye. His head is too easily turned by "mysterious and scarcely mortal girls" (with romantic names like Erminé and Jobina).

At thirteen, Josephine has a string of schoolgirl crushes that belie her reputation as "a siren," "a speed." However often she is jilted by Viking-like blonds with sad eyes, she remains certain that "life has innumerable beginnings." And whatever dams are placed in her way, "the overwhelming life in her" manages to explode. Until—"A Snobbish Story" exposes her as callously disloyal. "It is more fun to love someone than to be loved" is her admission of her fear of responsibility.

Josephine has acted out so many parts that self-identity eludes her, and her faked emotions finally backfire. When in the last story, "Emotional Bankruptcy," genuine passion comes her way, it leaves her cold. Munching on a candy after being kissed, she tells her would-be lover: "I don't feel anything . . . you're everything I've always wanted. But I've had everything." "Help me!" she implores him. It is the same cry that half-crazed Nicole utters in *Tender Is the Night* when she discovers a self in her she doesn't recognize.

Josephine's sudden illumination is not quite believable, and her final anguish clashes with the tone of the stories as a whole. But she has helped lead Fitzgerald to a clearing. In *Tender Is the Night*, he would move to a Faustian concept of tragedy that would contain "the ecstasy of ambition" he understood so well.

1973

Where the Center
Always Holds:
Stories by Brendan Gill

Like so many readers of the *New Yorker,* I have long admired
Brendan Gill as a writer of sharp, sophisticated apperceptions.
As that magazine's drama critic and long-time contributor of
short stories, he is a model of tempered urbaneness, contemporary
without ever being literal. But there is another Brendan Gill I might
never have known if I had missed reading this first collection of his
stories (not all from the *New Yorker*). This *alter* ego is essentially a
poet, with a poet's concern for *emotional* truth, for those tenuous
strands that hold together our fragmented beings and, for better or
worse, make us "whole." Being a deft craftsman as well (there are few
short-story writers who can say so much in a first paragraph), he can,
in a flip, spin tales with neat, paradoxical endings; but at his best, in
his gently ironical stories, the poet is the winner.

With all the archness of his title, there is little in *Ways of Loving* to
suggest John O'Hara's bitter views on the same subject. Mr. Gill's
touch is lighter, kinder; his conclusions more tentative. There are
echoes in his dialogues of I. Compton-Burnett's inverted comedies,
but the perversions of "domestic affections" he sees end in pathos

rather than shock. What he finds ironical is that "intimate" relationships can exist—and often do—on the meagerest fares of love. Mr. Gill's interest in "freaks" is minimal. With very few exceptions, his characters are free of fashionable aberrations; their inability to love or inspire love, it seems, is part of a common human flaw.

The stories read like a series of variations on a theme—the "ways" of *nearly* loving—and are best when they pinpoint a moment that marks a transition, a conversion, or its opposite, the fixed nature's point of no return. The human phenomenon, where the center always *holds*, is the whole story. "The End of an Exceptionally Short Affair" is a brief close-up of a pair of egocentric lovers: a middle-aged man still yearning for that one real "love" and a young girl avid for "experience." As each hugs his pride, the magic between them dies, aborted. In "The Fat Girl," his most spellbinding story, ego gratification takes on a more lurid form. Jeanne, the young secretary, is brutally murdered by her boy friend, and as the story opens the narrator suggests an unlikely link between the girl's fate and her "lazy, accommodating nature." As scenes from her life unfold, we see, in fact, how gluttony creates an inner void. Her murder becomes a senseless act that happens to people who themselves make nothing happen.

Though the Fat Girl is vividly portrayed in terms of an inert environment, Mr. Gill's characters generally escape obvious social classification. They are men and women before they are doctors, clubmen, dowagers, priests, farmhands, lonely widowers—trapped more by their characters than by their lives. Claire, in the novella "The Malcontents," goes through life vaguely sensing she has lost or missed something. A thwarted lesbian and wealthy divorcée, she has settled into a life of "togetherness" with her son and her dowager mother. The triad, constantly at sword's end with one another as they flit about from place to place, has its comic aspects (which Mr. Gill doesn't miss), but the circuitous story veers toward a pathetic ending—Claire's delusion, as she sheds her family, that at last she can claim her true identity.

More dazzling in its impact is "The Triumph," a wry little tale in which a small incident triggers confrontation with hidden feelings. An elderly mother and her middle-aged daughter, social snobs with reduced means, project an aura of near-perfect harmony as they set about preparing for their annual party. The one note of disagreement arises over the inclusion on their list of the daughter's newest acquaintance, a woman who gives the impression that "all her life she has done what she pleased." When the newcomer fails to measure up at the party, the mother's quiet outrage suddenly exposes the true nature of the mother-daughter relationship.

The lives of a widower and his spinster daughter are linked in a more subtle, mutually oppressive way in "The Sacrifice." Both have "long given up seeing each other clearly." But self-revelation comes when in a sharp moment of grief the daughter acknowledges that she has sacrificed nothing by remaining with her father: no one else wants or needs her.

The ache of failure, of rejection, comes up again and again, captured most luminously in the shorter stories. Where the predicaments are less universal or where "total" conversion is the subject, Mr. Gill's success is more limited. "Last Things," a scenariolike story of an improbable marriage, takes much too long to make its self-evident point. In "And Holy Ghost," Sister Louise's success in converting an agnostic boy is too matter-of-factly told to absorb that extra dimension of truth. And the most ambitious story in the book, "The Sunflower Kid," about a young Negro farmhand's Candide-like experiences, dissipates its power by an ending so tentative as to be meaningless.

The alternations of light and dark tones in the stories are part of the difficulty of Mr. Gill's style. At its best, the mixture strengthens rather than disrupts the story's unity. But in the less structured stories, it can also confuse his intent. There is, too, something not altogether "contemporary" (in the more limited sense of the word) in the way he encloses his characters in a self-contained world, allowing nothing external to impinge on their consciousness. To capture the "totality of existence," he must ignore a more common view of man as elusive and ever-changing. But, perhaps, the absence of love—or its masks—can be felt only by the poet who sees us "whole."

1974

God Bless You, Mr. Vonnegut

There was a time not too long ago when I desperately clung to Kurt Vonnegut's name. It was the one that came most readily to mind whenever I was asked who among the newest American writers would make the literary galaxy. Without racking my brain too much I could have come up with the names of other writers of equal reputation: Barth, Pynchon, Barthelme, and so on. Mr. Vonnegut's was the surest. One could admire the others, but the author of *Player Piano* and *God Bless You, Mr. Rosewater,* one *enjoyed.* And nothing in literature lasts that is not enjoyed. Not that Mr. Vonnegut's work was exactly cheering: with all its free-wheeling manner, it involved readers in a conspiracy of doom that was perversely calming—what's left to be done after the funeral? Long before "moonwalk" his imagination had sought a far-off planet from which to view the earthlings below. What he saw so simplified and enlarged the present moment that it could be grasped in its totality. From *Cat's Cradle* on he has been our cultural critic and guru.

A decade later, one can see he is not in a class with Orwell (whom he favors) or even with Twain (whom he resembles physically these days). As a social satirist he is too playful; the moral quality is muted in him—as it is in another writer of prophetic aspirations, William Saroyan—by a strain of deep sentiment that seeks release in laughter. Grim, ironic laughter for "atheist" Vonnegut, genial humor for earthy Saroyan. Mr. Rosewater/Vonnegut's desperate plea, "God damn it, you've got to be kind," would grate on the ear of the cocky young optimist of *My Name Is Aram.* And vice versa. To achieve a feeling of oneness with humankind, all Mr. Saroyan had to do was "remember that living people are as good as dead." That could do as a survival kit for the Depression years; it was hardly adequate for the surreal world after World War II and a writer who had actually seen living corpses as a prisoner of war. The idiom of the age ruled out positive thinking.

Other circumstances ruled it out as well. In *Wampeters, Foma & Granfalloons: (Opinions),* a provocative volume of articles, campus speeches, miscellaneous pieces and an interview, Mr. Vonnegut's self-revelations go beyond the "opinions" of the subtitle. At fifty-one, he is understandably eager to tell us who he is and why. But not being introspective by nature, he imagines that the book "shows [me] trying to tell the truth nakedly, without the ornaments of fiction." That is a "foma" (harmless untruth in Mr. Vonnegut's dictionary) that his fans will be quick to spot. Anyone who has watched him on the platform knows how well he doubles for Billy Pilgrim, fresh from the land of flying saucers, as he glides from earnestness into his very own blend of glib cynicism and ancient wisdom. So it goes.

But style is the man, as the saying goes, and along the way—as he ruminates on space programs, on the 1972 political conventions, on Richard M. Nixon or Hermann Hesse, on genocide in Biafra, or the systemization of human aspirations—there are capsule glimpses of the inner man. In his delightful "Yes, We Have No Nirvanas," he can, at the same time, epitomize the leader of Transcendental Meditation and suggest why he could never himself be among the quarter of a million followers of "the darling man": the Maharishi reminds him of "the euphoric men" at General Electric in Schenectady (where Mr. Vonnegut was a public relations man years ago) who "thought it was ridiculous for people to be unhappy, when there were so many things they could do to improve their lot." Mr. Vonnegut opts for Jesus on the spot.

With "the mysterious Mme. Blavatsky," on the other hand, Mr. Vonnegut is "charmed and amused." Her spooky spiritualism notwithstanding, "she brought wisdom from the East, which was very much needed. . . . If she garbled or invented some of that wisdom, she was doing no worse than other teachers have done."

There are degrees of danger in modern man's avid urge toward a "better" life; in Mr. Vonnegut's eyes, such gullibility assumes plaguelike proportions when manipulated by power-mad politicians, self-deceived heart and kidney transplanters, and technologists who have sold their souls to science. The word "soul" is not Mr. Vonnegut's word here, but what unleashes his wildest irony is the absence of something very much like it in Mr. Nixon's "spiritual" adviser, the man who indirectly helped design his "neo-Metternichian scheme for lasting world peace." "The single religion of the Winners," he notes, "is a harsh interpretation of Darwinism which argues that it is the will of the universe that only the fittest should survive."

If there are some too slight or cute items in the volume, the sardonic piece on the Republican National Convention ("In a Manner That Must Shame God Himself") more than makes up for it. And the *Playboy* interview, though shot through with "foma," has surprises. In a rare moment of unabashed compassion, Mr. Vonnegut tells the interviewer: "People are too good for this world." Earlier, he grows sublime as he urges the graduating class at Bennington to "believe in the most ridiculous superstition of all: that humanity is at the center of the universe, the fulfiller or the frustrater of the grandest dreams of God Almighty." Some pessimist.

Yet for Mr. Vonnegut (who admits to "depressions"), the apocalypse has physical reality. "The sun," he says, "is going to exhaust its fuel . . . the planet is surely dying." For a man with a background in physics and anthropology, that is short of hallucinatory. The gallows humor is more than an idiom of the age. At every turn, moral outrage meets with a deep fatality about a future in which good and evil themselves will be ground into a "system." In the end, like his characters, Mr. Vonnegut looks outside reality for help. "The only way in which Americans . . . can rescue their planet," he observes, "is through enthusiastic intimacy with works of their imagination." Ironically, only the imagination can keep the truth inviolate. God bless you, Mr. Vonnegut—and may the works of your imagination multiply.

1974

Realists of the Interior: Women Poets of Today

O nce there was Emily Dickinson, spinster, recluse, making poetry out of hoarded drama; there was Edna St. Vincent Millay, head in the clouds, yearning for renascence; and there was Marianne Moore, sage duenna in a tricornered hat, working her sly alchemy with words. Repressed, romantic, fastidious—together they merged into a portrait of the woman poet in America.

Now all that has changed. In the past decade or more a whole new breed of women poets has emerged, intent on effacing that outworn image. In another age, poetry's reality was elusive, indeterminate, like women's lives, and so a certain kind of poetic expression came naturally to women. Yet only now when a concrete and more explicit style prevails are women publishing poetry in feverish profusion. Women's Lib has undoubtedly played its part in making publishers aware of them. But even before the movement got started, poets like May Swenson, Denise Levertov, Daisy Aldan and Carolyn Kizer were articulating the new stance and drawing critical attention (regardless of their gender). Reading in three recently published anthologies* of

---

Psyche: The Feminine Poetic Consciousness. Edited by Barbara Segnitz and Carol Rainey; *Rising Tides: Twentieth-Century American Poets.* Edited by Laura Chester and Sharon Barba; *Mountain Moving Day: Poems by Women.* Edited by Elaine Gill.

women poets, one begins naturally enough by examining the so-called "feminine poetic consciousness"; one ends by rummaging for the poems that confront what is more important: Are women as women, using their authentic voices, mastering the poetic art?

"The young turn to poetry when the world becomes intolerable," writes Anaïs Nin in a brief, diagnostic introduction to *Rising Tides.* "It is the creative drug . . . the creative healer." And, indeed, colloquial and contemporary, the poems—read together—surface in a shower of words, dazzling in their directness, their sheer energy. No one is hoarding dramas anymore; if anything they are exorcising them: "I'm tired / of hand me downs / shut me ups . . . I'm / gonna spread out / over America / intrude / my proud blackness / all / over the place . . ." writes the gifted black poet Mari Evans. The new aggression women are experiencing is directed as much toward themselves—those unwanted selves—as toward a deluded world. Adrienne Rich's seventh book is titled *Diving into a Wreck* ("wreck" standing for the myths of womanhood); Anne Sexton's *Transformations* undercuts fantasy with a demonic thrust at a common source of our innocence: the fairy tale. And Sylvia Plath's *Ariel* poems read like a bitter parody of Shelley—the poet imprisoned in her concrete, inanimate world, courting mortality. "Out of the ash / I rise with my red hair / and I eat men like air," cries her Lady Lazarus in cynical defiance.

The theatrical effect of the nihilistic Plath verse (in which the depth of bitterness never quite matches the circumstances to be gleaned from the poems themselves) is echoed in the work of other poets with less stunning impact: "They were talking of their integrity and existential ennui / while the women ran out for six packs and had abortions / in the kitchen and fed the children and were auctioned off" is Marge Piercy's flamboyant way of presenting the man-woman relationship at its bleakest. The new candor can be brash and strident; it is unabashedly vulgar in its insistence on slang anatomical words. Yet its bawdiness can delight if it is alive and written with a true ear, as in Erica Jong's "Bitter Pills for Dark Ladies." Uninhibited language in itself is actually not offensive (it can reveal the underside of the mind); what is offensive is the lapses into the banal: "I keep looking for a man who will satisfactorily replace you / in my life" (addressed to Beethoven) is about as anti-poetic as one can get.

Realists of the interior (their own), the younger poets especially have absorbed the message of William Carlos Williams: they are thinking with their poems out of an immediate need. Though Sylvia Plath (their heroine) committed suicide and others have experienced psychotic states, they are essentially earthlings, committed to multifaceted life-styles (as their biographies attest). Recipients of poetry awards and grants, they have acquired status. And this may be the cause of a new unease, a self-consciousness. The intense awareness of self in poets like Miss Rich, Miss Sexton, Diane Wakoski and Margaret Atwood creates a painful yearning, not for rebirth in the Millayesque sense, but initial birth, the knowledge that one finally exists.

"Soon /," writes Miss Rich, "practice may make me middling perfect. I'll / dare inhabit the world / trenchant in motion as an eel . . ." Miss Sexton's exulting "Celebration of My Uterus" is positively Whitmanesque! Wary of lovers, husbands, fathers (and other male antagonists), these women sleep like "guerrilla fighters with one eye open for attack." In one Atwood poem, a "gentle husband" guards a paper bag that holds, along with an apple and a turnip, his wife's head, "the eyes closed."

These poets have come out of Freud but have left him behind. Their private guilts and anxieties are linked to larger evils like Vietnam and the lingering Nazi experience. Their "hallucinations"—a jumble of perceptions—derive from the nightmare of reality. If there is deadwood in these volumes (even from good poets), they are still a great bargain per page in terms of talent, energy and verbal power. Having had its "mountain moving day," "the feminine poetic consciousness" is due for some relief. When it picks up the dream and the alchemy again, it should play second fiddle to none.

1974

Bitches and Sad Ladies

A film critic recently observed that women as leading characters were fast disappearing from the screen. The rationale offered was that audiences today were divided between those who could not tolerate overly aggressive heroines and those who wanted women to be shown as victims. There being no model on which all could agree, it seemed safest to remove the heroine entirely from view.

Luckily, this state of affairs does not hold for fiction, where women protagonists continue to flourish. In the novels and short stories of women writers especially, the heroine (or anti-heroine, if you will) is gaining new status as she sheds the romantic emblems, crude fantasies and faded blueprints that male writers still impose on her. Nowadays, it is often the nondescript, unexceptional woman who is seen from the inside out, through a consciousness better described as a labyrinth than a stream.

In its generous sampling of stories by talented and prolific women writers, Pat Rotter's anthology *Bitches and Sad Ladies* provides a convenient laboratory for examining the new heroine and speculating on her composite image. Miss Rotter herself sees contemporary women in the dual guise of "bitch" and "sad lady." "Independent/dependent. Aggressive/passive. Subject/object. All it takes to make a bitch out of a sad lady is some healthy anger and a growing ego." It is a neat formula, but it doesn't explain why the "bitch" is such a rarity in these stories. To my mind, there are only two real bitches in the volume—and both are exposed with irony and sly wit. Una, in Julia O'Faolain's Freud/Sade-inspired story, "Man in the Cellar," settles a score with her husband—but loses him—when she literally shackles and enslaves him in their cellar. And the self-centered academic Mary Chimes, in Cynthia Ozick's hard-headed tale "An Education," gives every priority to her career and, as a result, loses her baby. If anger "liberated" these two women, the writers ask, who's the better for it?

The "sad ladies," on the other hand, are not wholly without romantic illusions—though romance has long since vanished from their lives. Miss Rotter notes how "love can sometimes be a crippling affliction." Astonishing, indeed, how many of these thirty-five stories take us inside doctors' offices and other cold, impersonal places! (Does this mean the body is the last stronghold to crumble before the "new order"?) Writers like Joyce Carol Oates, Gail Godwin, Anne Sexton and others in the anthology show new awareness of the fact that the rational self is vulnerable to physiological pressures and is easily betrayed. Without trying to *explain,* they show us the fissures in the psyche, the "interstices" (Miss Godwin uses the word as her title) that cause havoc—not true madness but the self's fragmentation, its "crippling."

Many of the stories deal with the crushing weight of indecision—that limbo state which Erica Jong identifies as "fear of flying." Better than most of her contemporaries, Joyce Carol Oates has mastered the tone and posture of the new anxiety, the vague unease. The heroines of her novels and stories are not afraid to act, but having acted on impulse and out of character are haunted thereafter by a sense of their own unreality. In "The Lady With the Pet Dog," her heroine has all the aggressiveness an adultress needs but, lacking courage of another kind, succumbs to "spiritual glamour"—a joyless form of bovaryism.

Self-alienation, for these writers, never takes a comic turn, as it does in the novels of Iris Murdoch. In the parablelike stories of Glenda Adams's "The Hollow Woman" and Anne Sexton's "The

Letting Down of the Hair," it skirts social satire to paint a terrifying inner void. On the threshold of freedom, the women in many of these stories negate life instead of affirming it. A woman camera-bug, in Rosellen Brown's ominous "Good Housekeeping," reorders the visible everyday world with a totalitarian disregard for the human element. Another woman, a would-be artist, in Carol Emshwiller's story, complains: "Reality is . . . very abstract . . . doesn't have much form." She finds art more fulfilling than life. And a woman poet, in Gail Godwin's delicate and powerful story, callously locks an unhappy experience into her work, pretending it never happened.

In this often stifling, interior world—mostly conveyed with realistic power—there is only a trace of the male presence. There are vaguely realized (because vaguely known) lovers; violent housemates; remote husbands who hope their wives' wild fantasies (like mailing letters to their husbands about their lovers) will just go away; doctors and psychiatrists, intent on inflicting pain and; now and then, an emblematic male out of a vengeful sexual fantasy. Is it possible, one wonders, that men are becoming less important in women's lives? Are the "fissures" and "interstices" setting up barriers? Or is the problem something more complex, involving the intransigence of men and of society?

Though many of the stories hint at this last point, one seemed particularly direct, without being polemical. Neither "bitch" nor "sad lady," the heroine of Sherry Sonnett's "Dreamy" sets out to embrace total Freedom. She leaves home, removes all traces of her past life, abandons all relationships and responsibilities. Alone, in her Walter Mitty dream, she waits for the time when "My life will have shape and form. My needs and expectations and desires will coincide perfectly with what my life provides. I will have everything." The tone is dry, controlled. The woman knows that the dream must remain in suspension until it finds a true echo in the outside world. There is no disputing that view.

1975

The World of
William Saroyan

What can one say about William Saroyan that he himself cannot say better? Does one need to analyze a rainbow? Should one try to explicate Cézanne? Does it really enhance our enjoyment of a work of Mozart or Chopin to explain how they achieve their effects? Saroyan has a way of defeating his critics even before they begin. And this is why, after an astonishingly prolific career spanning more than forty years, Saroyan has remained virtually untouched by literary historians or critics and why to this day there is no standard edition of his works.

That fact in itself is my challenge in venturing to explore the Saroyan phenomenon and, by bringing together the various threads of his achievement, to reveal him to readers in a new way.

Like so many others, undoubtedly, I have been reading Saroyan or seeing his plays in bits and pieces over the years. (I recall that I wrote an article titled "Saroyan Prescribes 'The Time of Your Life' " in my college magazine.) To this day you will find his work in all kinds of publications: in the *Ladies' Home Journal,* the *New York Times* (Op-Ed or Sunday Book Review), *Harper's,* the *Atlantic,* the *New Yorker* and even *TV Guide.* Recently the Shirtsleeve Theatre produced a new play of his, *The Rebirth Celebration of the Human Race at Artie*

Zabala's Off Broadway Theatre, and in the fall of 1975 John Houseman's Acting Company brought us that longtime classic, his 1939 Pulitzer Prize play, *The Time of Your Life.* Not to forget the Armenian Diocese's production in the winter of 1975 of a new play, *The Armenians,* which some of us were fortunate to catch in its short run. An autobiographical work, *Sons Come and Go but Mothers Hang in Forever,* was published in the summer of 1976.

We listen to Saroyan, we watch, we read—now with a sense of enchantment, now with disappointment (no writer can be so prolific and remain always in top form), but most often with refreshment—as he restores harmony and wholeness to our sight—and then we go on to something else: usually these days to something more involved, full of confusion and dissonance and unresolvable, sticky modern problems. In this intermittent awareness of Saroyan, we tend to glimpse and remember certain repeated motifs, in themselves not always so significant: we invariably seize on the *ethnic* subject—the wacky uncles and cousins, the sly old-country humor, the desperate need to be moral about life. Or, depending on our taste and inclination, we will wallow in—or be put off by—his unabashed belief in the goodness of man, by his childlike delight in being alive and disconnected with the larger world and its turmoil. Still others—the critics, for instance—will wonder that there is still so much vitality left in the old boy, when his younger contemporaries, J. D. Salinger, Jack Kerouac, Carson Mc-Cullers and Truman Capote, either are dead or have virtually given up writing.

It is only when one reads Saroyan continuously over a period of time that one can come to a true estimate of his stature as a writer, apart from the particular things one loves in him. Only then can one begin to find an explanation for his inexhaustible creativity and for the secret of his durability in this somber era of the twentieth century.

Saroyan has written reams about his own work in his prefaces to his stories and plays, most of it more distracting than useful to a critic. But nothing he has written is as revealing as the statement he makes in the preface to his ballet-play, "The Great American Goof," from his 1941 book *Razzle-Dazzle.*

"Nobody other than myself," he wrote, "seems to understand that the world is not real. That in reality there is no such thing as the world. There is, of course, but I mean for all practical purposes; when I say practical I mean poetic and wonderful. The world which everyone other than myself seems to have identified and accepted as the World is in reality a figment in a nightmare of an idiot. No one could possibly create anything more surrealistic and unbelievable than the world which everyone believes is real and is trying hard to inhabit. *The job of art, I say, is to make a world which can be inhabited.*"

He goes on to say in this preface that while he ignores the world deliberately, he keeps a clear eye on it all the time. "The style in our day," he continues, "is to save the world in every poem we write. . . . But probably the most any man can ever save or has a right to save is himself." "What I say is, what world? Where do you see any world?"

You cannot be in Saroyan's presence for any length of time without realizing that in his own life, his own person, he has remained true to the beliefs and ideals that informed his work from the beginning. There was never a character more Saroyanesque than Saroyan himself today. If anything, he is more emphatically himself than he ever was. With this difference: As a young man there was brashness and bravado in the way he let his faith be known. The world had still to humble him—he was aware that it would, for the world spared no one, least of all the sensitive. Uttered in his late sixties, the brash remark (if there is one) is followed by a knowing chuckle, as if he were not denying what he said but winking at the way he was saying it, only to emphasize his point: that life has meaning, that art and literature are the best means we have of expressing that meaning, that a dignified survival for any of us, but especially for the artist, matters more than anything else.

Let me digress here for a moment to tell a little about the Saroyan I saw in the summer of 1975 in his Paris surroundings. I was traveling with my sister, the writer Anna Balakian, and her daughter Suzanne, in both of whom Saroyan found kindred spirits. Never solemn, least of all when he is mouthing solemn truths, Saroyan at once put us at ease: a great talker, he is also a good listener, and because he seems to sense what in particular will interest those in his company, there is continual give and take. In his simply, casually furnished walk-up apartment near the Opéra, where he spends several months of the year (those times he is away from Fresno, California), the books and papers are neatly piled, ready to be referred to. Drinking tea with him there, or later over Schweppes (he hardly ever touches alcohol these days), or casually talking over instant coffee in the Paris office of the *New York Times*—on all these occasions, he appeared the soul of affability, spreading the contagion of his warmth, of his unfailing good humor.

Not that the reflective, the serious side was missing: talking about his new plays (and he has a stack of them which he will not show to publishers or producers), he deplores the present state of the American theater, which he blames essentially on the commercialization of the arts in general, and also on agents, editors and reviewers. There are hints of outrage, of anger held in check—for he remains a man who cares. But underneath it all is a benign acceptance of life's vicissitudes if not of their power to crush the individual. Unencumbered by material possessions, still keeping alive memories of the Fresno-Armenian oasis of his early youth, while at the same time never losing hold on the present moment, with whatever demands it makes on him, he is a new kind of mystic, a free spirit who knows life's true worth and has retained his zest for doing what he can to cause it to be revealed.

In Saroyan's denial of the world there is none of the elitist escapism of the expatriates of the twenties. Saroyan is not involved in any experimental literary group; he simply does his work, looks around, communicates *silently* with the natives (for though he understands French, he makes little effort to speak it). He waves to the little boy leaning out of a window across the street and waits to see him wave back—a sign of their common humanity. If anything, on this alien soil, his American quality is more than ever pronounced. It is reflected not only in his dress, which is casual and comfortable (even baggy), in his Western American accent and extravagance of expression, but in more subtle ways that speak of his need always to be himself, to put the most ordinary stranger at ease, to deflate pomposity, and to expect nothing less than the impossible. Indeed, one is tempted to conclude that the source of Saroyan's optimism is his assimilation of the American stance—the *original* American, of course, with his inborn faith in "life, liberty and the pursuit of happiness."

But if that alone were its source, why would he stand out as a maverick? The unaffiliated beatniks and flower children of the fifties, racing their way on the road, their backs turned on an oppressive Establishment, seemed also to be created in the original American mold. What essential lack of faith led them down the road to disillusionment, with specious escape in drugs, in asocial acts? If Saroyan's optimism is more firmly embedded, one suspects it is because it derives not from escape from the self but from head-on confrontation with it. Those wacky and unreconstructed Armenian uncles and cousins, those misfits and losers on whom Saroyan centers his affection, are never romanticized "noble savages," as some critics have suggested. Think of the idealistic father, the unpublished poet in *My Heart's in the Highlands,* or Homer's mother in *The Human Comedy,* and all those innumerable Saroyan children: innocents they may be and quite unsophisticated in the ways of the world, but they have manners and insights that suggest they relate to their fellow men: they are too innately cultured to be mistaken for "savages."

In one of his earliest stories in *The Daring Young Man on the Flying Trapeze,* Saroyan says:

"I cannot resist the temptation to mock any law which is designed to hamper the spirit of man."

The word to watch for in that sentence is "spirit." He wants the spirit of man, what renders him human, to be protected from the corrupting pressures of society. And the proof of this lies in the fact that these special rebels of Saroyan—call them "spiritual rebels"—do not deny the home, repudiate the family or community: they do not shun their neighbors or denounce the pleasures of simple fellowship. Quite the contrary, Saroyan's people seem to exist for the purpose of establishing the fraternity of man.

And then there is, of course, Saroyan's ethnic dimension. Paradoxical though it may seem, no influence on Saroyan has done more to reinforce his claim as an American writer than his Armenian heritage and background.* (I speak here again of an earlier American style, not the contemporary, which has absorbed so many foreign influences.) Saroyan's childhood experiences among his uninhibited, colorful Fresno-Armenians have left a significant impact not only on his character but on the very manner of his storytelling. I refer to that often long-winded, indirect manner of the Eastern *massal* or long tale (e.g., "The Thousand and One Arabian Nights"), always at its best when it reflects the idiosyncrasy of the teller's personality. If in Saroyan this does not stand out as a foreignism, it is because it blends so well with another tradition, the American Western oral tradition (used so effectively before him by writers like Mark Twain and Ring Lardner), which Saroyan absorbed through his reading and environment. In addition, as a child in the circle of his extended family, he fell under the spell of the fable, which in turn drew him to allegory and that extra dimension of reality which as a young idealist he set out to discover. Here again, an influence in his *American* environment turns the fable's impact into a moral force. Though he often refers to himself as a mystic (and speaks of the *mystery* of religion), the specific religious references in his work are of the Presbyterian church where he attended Sunday School and briefly sang in the choir. To this day, he sings these hymns with affectionate reverence.

There were other moral forces in his early years that combined the American and Armenian influences. There was the example of his im-

---

*In a recent review in the *New York Times Book Review,* Edward Hoagland takes note of the fact that Saroyan "has been a profoundly, innovatively 'ethnic' writer—one of the very first in America." What needs to be added in this connection is that Saroyan was the first ethnic writer to carry the ethnic element into the universal. It is in the naturalness and ease with which he achieves this transmutation that Saroyan's originality lies.

migrant widowed mother, struggling to keep the family alive; there was the historic proof of man's tenacity to survive in the heroic story of his own Armenian people. The Armenians' suffering and endurance through the centuries inevitably fused in his mind with the agony of a world on the brink of world war and the deep gloom of America's demeaning Depression years. The years when he was emerging as a writer—the middle thirties—were a time of leveling off: white-collar workers, laborers, professionals mingled in a common pursuit for subsistence. Economic pressures drew people closer together as they sought solace in friendship, relief in humor, and hope in love. Having been brought up to cherish these things, Saroyan sought from his earliest stories to bring a more mystical apprehension to the American Dream. He wrote in 1934: "I am a propagandist, and in this very story I am trying to restore man to his natural dignity and gentleness. I want to restore man to himself. I want to send him from the mob to his own body and mind. I want to lift him from the nightmare of history to the calm dream of his own soul, the true chronicle of his kind."

Rereading *The Daring Young Man on the Flying Trapeze,* one is struck by the essential solemnity underlying the work as a whole: the cosmic consciousness and the rhetoric it unleashes contain echoes of Sherwood Anderson and Thomas Wolfe, with an occasional departure into the tight-lipped Hemingway. The characteristic Saroyan humor has not yet emerged from under the weight of romantic naturalism. But with successive volumes of his stories—*Inhale, Exhale, Three Times Three, Little Children,* and *My Name Is Aram*—Saroyan learned to detach himself from his characters, or, rather, to keep a certain distance from them, in order to empathize with a broader spectrum of humanity.

Reviewers of these early books were generally charmed by the variety and appeal of his ethnic characters, by the refreshing absence of political and sociological preaching in a time when "the movement" was on everyone's lips, by the warm-hearted humor and the hope for humanity his stories generated. Later, the more literal-minded of the critics grew impatient, even bored, since instead of inventing new plots and dramatic situations Saroyan reworked his material, improvising variations on certain basic themes.

Parenthetically, let me say here that Saroyan (who loves music of every sort) loves particularly to listen to Chopin; this he does in Paris on an ancient victrola that leaves much of the music to one's imagination. Interesting—because I have thought of his stories in terms of music like Chopin's, which moves from a fixed center toward limits that are foreordained yet curiously liberating in their essential sameness. In the preface to a short play, "Opera, Opera," he wrote: "The truth of art is the truth of emotion, not intellect. Emotion and intellect are essentially or eventually inseparable, and the quality of one depends on the quality of the other." Behind that emotion is a fixed vision of the human potential—an ideal—which most of us, in the process of living, often lose sight of. To keep that vision alive, he repeatedly places before our eyes fragments of what he calls "a world which can be inhabited."

"What was the human race I discovered in Fresno?" he asks in "The Home of the Human Race." "It was my family, my neighbors, my friends, the teachers at the school, the classmates, the strangers in the streets, and myself, most of all myself." And he goes on: "Were the strangers any good at all? Was it possible to believe them at all? They *were* good: good and hopeless, and that is why I discovered art, for I did not want them to be hopeless." Only through art, he knew, could their dignity be preserved.

Saroyan's innocents are not only children—though children are among his best creations. Among the adult innocents are the nonconformists, nonmilitant eccentrics, like the uncle who decided to grow pomegranates in the desert, undaunted by warnings of inevitable failure; they are also the unconditioned young people who let their hearts dictate their actions, like the young girl in a prison kitchen who responds to a prisoner's anguished call in his play *Hello, Out There!* They are the "losers" who hang on, like the writer Rock Wagram in his 1951 novel of that name, living by the "lies of his art that wink and tell him he is the one." But best of all, though sometimes barely believable, are the deliberate innocents—the free spirits who turn their backs on the materialistic world to cultivate compassion, beauty, love, wholeness, humor.

Even more than courage, it is humor that sustains these free spirits. Humor in Saroyan's human family is a saving grace, the balm that heals, the lifeline that leaves fear and disenchantment behind. Again and again, the realist and the mystic go hand in hand to create a sense of absurdity in the differences that separate the mundane world from his own way of seeing it. Through his ever-present sense of man's mortality, Saroyan keeps his eye fixed on the natural world, that rich, true, earthy place on the other side of the artificial Human Comedy, where there are no roles to be enacted and a person's true style is allowed to emerge.

It is not my intention here to account for the repeated failures Saroyan suffered in the years following World War II when he turned from short-story writing to the novel. With the exception of *The Human Comedy,* which he originally wrote as a Hollywood script, he seemed not to have been challenged by the novel form. *The Adventures of Wesley Jackson* was a mild experiment in the mock-heroic novel, but in neither *Rock Wagram* (which deals with the age-old quest of the son for his father) nor *Laughing Matter* (an O'Neillesque family saga) was there any truly innovative writing. In the novel form he could not project the large canvas of people who were his metaphor for humanity; nor could he place his personal stamp in terms of style. And in the end these are the things that matter in Saroyan.

From a critic's point of view, it would have profited Saroyan not to have published some of these novels: they not only gave him a bad press but they obscured the true thrust of his genius. When he turned to drama in 1939, writing right off one of the classic plays of the modern American theater, *The Time of Your Life,* he announced his intention of being an innovator in the theater. And the critics stood in attention. Though O'Neill and Thornton Wilder (in *Our Town*) had broken through some of the naturalistic barriers of the American theater, nothing quite so informal and spontaneous had happened on the American stage before Saroyan came along. Unconcerned about character motivation in the traditional sense; indifferent to social manners, raw dramatic situations or abnormal drives, Saroyan sought to turn the theater into "the last arena in which all is always possible." The stage would hereafter become his true home; using himself only in bits and pieces through his various creations, he would find it easier in this medium to achieve the detachment that art requires. Saroyan's stage would become a place where human beings could shed the false roles life had assigned them, in order to play whatever roles they might choose themselves. And so Saroyan's Beautiful People were born—a phrase which he coined. (Unfortunately, this would later become a synonym for the jet set!)

While his Pulitzer Prize play *The Time of Your Life* and his *My Heart's in the Highlands* (also of that year) were well received, his subsequent plays had mixed reviews. Though beguiled by the poetry and humor in his work, there were those who deplored his excessive optimism in a world on the brink of chaos and his lack of theatrical style and form. In the forties and fifties, a Saroyan play no sooner opened than it closed. There was no Off-Broadway to speak of, and the commercial theater had little appeal for an individualist like Saroyan who insisted on doing things his own way. At one point, in the flush of his success, Saroyan sought to establish a Saroyan theater. He gave away tickets to preview performances of *The Beautiful People,* which he himself directed and produced. But that fragile, tender little play about a family's mad whims growing out of their compassionate natures was not exactly for Broadway palates. Before the total absence of a dramatic plot, Brooks Atkinson of the *New York Times* grew fidgety. Why, he asked, didn't Saroyan write plays with specific conclusions? Why was he not *theatrical?*

In truth, Saroyan was being theatrical, but in a way that the theater had forgotten to be. Long before the modern theater came along, the theater combined pageantry with allegorical abstractions; it told a story in terms of humanity at large, and any action there presented was representational and symbolic. Saroyan's theater, with some exceptions, borrows from the Morality play of pre-Shakespearean days in its indifference to logical, literal action, if not its rather orthodox moral strictures. A character in a Saroyan play is never himself alone, with a particular destiny, but rather the essence of a human being with only one possible destiny—living and dying. This is the reason his plays offer no specific conclusions, but only repeated affirmations.

One cannot, of course, overlook two other important sources— again indigenous ones—from which Saroyan's plays derive: namely, American vaudeville, with its variety of visual and aural happenings and swift changes of pace and mood, and the silent movies, with their big-hearted clowns (one thinks especially of Charlie Chaplin) and the inner fantasy world to which these films spoke. These simple art forms must have helped him to abandon the more conventional stage techniques and turn to the rhythmic patterns and poetic associations which his themes required.

One concession to realism which Saroyan made in the two 1939 plays (as he had in his stories) was in placing his action against the backdrop of the current world crisis and the Depression with which the country was understandably obsessed. But with *The Beautiful People* (1941), that dimension was removed as Saroyan's extravagant whimsy contemplated the gentle consequences of impracticalness: in this case a teen-ager who intends to write novels consisting only of words he understands and who therefore begins by writing a one-word novel, *Tree,* and his sister who not only will not kill mice but insists on feeding them and giving them shelter. Along with several shorter works—among them *Across the Board on Tomorrow Morning*—this play marked the beginning of Saroyan's break with the naturalistic theater.

I think it speaks for the classic dimensions of *The Time of Your Life* that two generations since it was written it is still being revived by repertory companies, along with Chekhov, Ibsen and O'Neill plays. Seeing it again recently, I recognized that it was not a flawless play—flawlessness, by the way, is something which Saroyan avoids if possible, since it hampers the creative process—but it is a play that forcefully captures an image of America that Saroyan has always held in reverence and that at this distance still remains irresistible and poignant.

Set in "an American place," as he calls it, "a honky-tonk bar" in San Francisco, it is a play of contradictions that denies human conditioning. Each of his characters, like performers in a variety show, appears in quickly recognizable guise—the quasi-cynical bartender, the lonely prostitute, the young gambler, the lover, the cowboy, the failed comedian, the bored, passive drunk. Life has fixed them all into molds, though not too finally; the true self, the soul—Saroyan shows—keeps surfacing, refusing to be stamped out. In the central character of Joe, the philosopher-poet who is moved to do good but has become too effete by a life of ease to be effective in action, Saroyan suggests a cogent analogy with the America of his day; he dilutes his criticism, however, by the presence on the scene of the comic folk-figure Kit Carson, in whose soul is concealed the archetypical American adventurer. It is Carson who recognizes at the moment of danger the counter meaning and consequence of the play's theme, "in the time of your life, live—so that in that good time there shall be no ugliness or death for yourself or for any life your life touches . . ." Carson is instinctively ready to act in the defense of the individual, against indignities to his *spirit*.

Though the realistic dimension in Saroyan's plays is never wholly absent, he has in recent years gravitated more and more away from the problems and crises of our time which lie at the source of the contemporary playwright's despair. Instead, he has become absorbed in uncovering small but significant proofs in the actions and relations of people that give away their essential humanness. Though the cosmic overtone is always there, an absence of intellectually graspable imagery makes them "metaphysical" only in flashes. His 1949 play *Don't Go Away Mad* is a "waiting" play that predates Samuel Beckett's *Waiting for Godot* by four years. It is ostensibly a play about a miscellaneous group of men in a hospital ward waiting to die. But, unlike Beckett's pathetic tramps, Didi and Gogo, whose lives have been reduced to grotesque and boring routines, Saroyan's crew finds itself with a heightened sense of life. One of them, an illiterate black, asks to have the dictionary read to him from beginning to end; another listens intently all day to Mozart; while still another watches with near-blind eyes the miracle of a rainbow across San Francisco Bay. For the duration of the play, at least, we believe in them and in their awareness of the goodness of life. Their faith in its infinite possibilities to the end dissipates their fear of death. Though a beautiful play to read, I cannot imagine that it will ever be produced for contemporary audiences. For while we appear ready to accept the extreme nihilism of a Beckett, we are still quite unprepared to accept so pure a vision of earthly beatitude.

When, in 1958, *The Cave Dwellers* (perhaps Saroyan's most original play) was produced on Broadway, Harold Clurman called it "sugared existentialism." Again the same complaint: it was threadbare of plot, and there was no confrontation with evil and pain. Saroyan's answer appeared in the introduction of the printed version of the play:

"Every playwright," he wrote, "creates a human race. The truth of his race does not lie in its resemblance to the real human race. It lies in his skill as a playwright, in his measure as a man. I cannot mind that I am accused of not hating the human race. As long as I am willing to go on being a member of that race, it goes against both nature and truth for me to hate it."

Saroyan's plea here, as in the countless plays he has written since and continues to write to this day, is for the artist's inalienable right to create his own vision of truth. In *The Cave Dwellers* Saroyan envisions (indeed celebrates) the possibility of a world in which there is no need for violence, because goodness has triumphed over evil—and by goodness, I should explain, Saroyan never means the readily acceptable virtues but a natural sensitivity that makes a person put himself in another's painful predicament or destiny. In his play he pictures that world graphically as rising out of the ruins—here seen as a broken-down, abandoned theater (an appropriate image, since in this world we all play our parts)—where a troupe of unemployed actors have taken shelter. It is another kind of "waiting" play. Two of the characters have given themselves royal titles, King and Queen (parts for which they were once well known), and represent human beings waiting to come to their rightful inheritance—the kingdom of Earth.

Somewhat more demanding and bewildering is the symbolism of *Jim Dandy: Fat Man in a Famine* (an earlier play), which takes place inside an eggshell in which are seen the ruins of a Public Library. In a dark cave appear two frightened children, a disengaged staircase, a saloon and a small jail. There is a poet seeking the Holy Grail, a librarian dressed like Cleopatra, a convict who claims he is everybody's friend, and a rich fat man who is dressed like a tramp. It is a play to challenge the best imagination of directors. In this evocation of the meaning of rebirth, there is endless color, sound, motion, and comic invention. "I never knew," says one of the characters (Fishkin) in a wistful monologue at the end of the play, "that it was not my mother and father who brought me forth. I never knew until this instant that I did not come here Fishkin! I came here *any* man to *act* my part, to *create* my role, to be whomsoever I should choose to be. How wrong, how wrong to learn so simple a thing so late!"

In one of the innumerable autobiographical interludes Saroyan has published in the past fifteen years, he writes about Beckett's *Waiting for Godot:* "This is not the only play, and if waiting is all we actually do, there are other ways of waiting, other ways to forget that we are in fact waiting and finally other ways to give over to being seized rather than to seize."

The overall impact of these fragments of autobiography—*Here Comes, There Goes You Know Who, One Day in the Afternoon of the World, Days of Life and Death and Escape to the Moon,* among others—suggests indeed that in middle age Saroyan has not abandoned his dynamic view of life. He is among the very few living writers whose vision has not become blurred by the absurdity of the modern world. "There is more simple gladness in every day I reach than ever before in life," he wrote in 1963 in *Not Dying*. Looking back on the "bad dream" (not explained) he had in 1955 when he thought his "time was up," he rejoices in the return of his creative energies. In his Paris apartment, in the company of his teen-age son and daughter, the writer comes suddenly to the full limit of himself, translating his art into his life. Now more fully in control, he writes as a discipline, to keep in training, as it were, with an air of disconcern as to whether he publishes what he writes.

"My writing after I had written it probably changed me for the better," he tells his son, "and to that extent it might also have changed the human race for the better, but the best change in me happened *while* I was writing. . . . When you work at the making of a new piece of writing, you gradually put away from yourself a lot of trash that is in your nature. You concentrate so intensely that in a sense you leave your body entirely, although it's there all the time. Your spirit, or *the* spirit, takes over—not for long: the spirit doesn't need a lot of time; it certainly doesn't need forever. It operates entirely in the instant, now, canceling time as we understand it."

That is as revealing a statement as Saroyan has made of the special relation he has maintained, or striven to maintain, toward his art. As Joe says to Kit Carson in *The Time of Your Life:* "Living is an art. It's not bookkeeping. It takes a lot of rehearsing for a man to get to be himself." In William Saroyan's world, the fact and the fiction have merged. His own truest convert, he earnestly—and joyously—continues to make it *a place which can be inhabited.*

1976

A Day of One's Own: Eudora Welty

Aweek before it was announced that she had won the Pulitzer Prize for her novel *The Optimist's Daughter,* Eudora Welty woke up one morning to find herself a local "celebrity," with her name on billboards and in neon lights. In a long career never lacking in honors, it was a new kind of public/private tribute devised by proud fellow-Mississippians—and it went to everyone's heart, including the publicity-shy author's: for a full week (May 1-6) in her hometown of Jackson a whopping "Eudora Welty Celebration" was staged as part of the tenth annual Mississippi Arts Festival. An ingenious idea which pooled the resources of some one thousand enterprising committee members throughout the state and brought together a multitude of the writer's friends, it spotlighted the uniqueness of Miss Welty's career in American letters.

After a week of incessant rain, the sun beamed in recognition as Governor William Waller, standing beside Miss Welty in the Old Capitol's House of Representatives (where Jefferson Davis once spoke), proclaimed May 2 "Eudora Welty Day" for the entire state. Some five hundred fans of the novelist, among them schoolchildren and college students who had taken time from classes to attend the ceremonies, heard the Governor praise "the nation's foremost lady of letters . . . a woman of quiet dignity and charm. . . ."

Amid the clatter of radio and television equipment, photographers and such, Miss Welty in a pink dress sat quietly, obviously pleased, her blue eyes as unguarded as a young girl's. Later, in grateful response to the Governor's words and a standing ovation, she expressed wonder at the whole event: "If anything like this has ever been done to another author," she quipped, "then I think we can beat them." There were chuckles, and everyone relaxed—as everyone always does in Miss Welty's presence.

Before reading from her recent epiclike novel *Losing Battles,* she told her listeners: "Just think of it as voices." And, once past the lyrical beginning, she threw herself into the work, acting out all the parts with the greatest relish. So complete was her identification with her characters that she might have been sitting in a room with them. The "voices" grew familiar: garrulous, lovable Eudora Welty characters in high-comedy situations, enveloped by a deeply humane, poetic comprehension.

Though other local talent had its day in Jackson's grand Coliseum and surrounding fair grounds—with such outside stars as Renata Tebaldi, Edward Villella and Vikki Carr helping capture a record attendance of 150,000—the first two days of the Festival were Miss Welty's own. On exhibit at the Department of Archives and History were her manuscripts, letters from editors, and a scrapbook with samplings of her reviews from over thirty years. A closed-circuit television special featured dramatizations of her stories by local actors and an illuminating "conversation" with local critic Frank Hains. In a little church converted into a theater, a select audience saw the New Stage Theater's delightful adaptation of her comic extravaganza *The Ponder Hea·t.*

For the visitor from the East, the "celebration" had a fairy-tale quality. Writers in America are not supposed to be famous and happy at the same time: the "literary life" so often engenders tense, semitragic figures with glossy fronts that cover up a multitude of frustrations. Yet here was a writer perfectly attuned to her milieu, the lilt in her voice and simplicity of her manner giving her away as no words could. No gloss. No front. Only a sharp, intense responsiveness, a feeling of comradeship.

At a party in her family home (where she now lives alone, not too far from two adoring nieces and a sisterly sister-in-law) the rooms are aglow with the tremendous affection she inspires. "It's been like a funeral," she laughs, pointing to the flowers, the messages, the casseroles from solicitous neighbors. Her guests include distinguished literary agent Diarmuid Russell, her earliest editors Mary Louise Aswell and Lewis Simpson, her most gifted prótegé, the novelist Reynolds Price, a favorite author Ross Macdonald, and all the doting cosmopolite friends she has come to know from her annual visits to New York. As the talk shifts from old times to new happenings (not least the Watergate affair), not once does Miss Welty appear weary or bored or out of it.

Her equanimity and "positive feelings" have their source undoubtedly in a happy early childhood, but also in the fact, as she put it in a recent interview, that her work "has always landed safely and among friends." Indeed the letters on exhibit show that the first two stories she submitted found immediate publication in a little magazine in Ohio. Two years later, in 1938, Robert Penn Warren was seeking her out for the prestigious *Southern Review* and Ford Madox Ford's encouragement was firing the young writer with ambition. The one dissenting note came from a New York editor who complained there was no "market" for a volume of short stories and urged her to write novels instead. The novels were eventually produced, but not before her now classic volumes of stories *A Curtain of Green* and *The Wide Net* won critical acclaim in the early 1940s.

Because the act of creating is a major joy in her life, Miss Welty feels no need to leave Jackson for long periods. The "experiences" are right there, waiting to be absorbed. Like Henry James's ideal writer, she is "blessed with the faculty which when you give an inch takes an ell . . . one of the people on whom nothing is lost."

"Place has the most delicate control over character," she has written; "location pertains to feeling." The "regionalism" attributed to her has given her work not only its rich texture but the contours of a separate world to hold up against the eternal one, that great mirror where qualities and flaws stand out in true proportion. But most of all, it has blessed her with her vivid Mississippians, with their immense sense of the singularity of people. "The living presence" of the individual which Eudora Welty's work all but sanctifies is in part a tribute to their human dimensions; in turn, by putting their very essence into her books, she has given them a surer sense of their own identity. But only a writer of stature could transform a city from a "crossroad of the South" to virtually a crossroad of the world.

1973

PART THREE

Crossing the Ethnic Barrier

One of the most widely discussed books in recent years was the autobiographical chronicle of the American critic Norman Podhoretz. As the provocative brashness of the title announces, *Making It* is the candid confessions of a writer who admits that he desired fame and power. Though he came by his rewards honestly as the boy wonder of the New York Literary Establishment in the early 1950s and as editor, at thirty-three, of the influential Jewish magazine *Commentary,* Podhoretz might have foreseen the barrage of criticism his book aroused. Everybody may love a success story, but not everybody, it seems, least of all literary critics, is ready to admit that success—like life, liberty and happiness—is a legitimate American pursuit. And, as if to equate success with the American Dream were not bold enough, Podhoretz gave nothing less than three cheers to the whole venture, admitting few pitfalls· on the way and never so much as a polite regret. As he tells it, the story of his climb from the ghetto of Brownsville in Brooklyn to prominence in the world of American letters seems all too easy. And in the absence of soul-searching, his immodesty becomes an easy target of ridicule.

Yet the book has an importance beyond Podhoretz's own understanding of what was unique in his experience. In their agitation over the writer's advertisements of himself, few of his critics concerned themselves, even in passing, with what to me is the book's most interesting feature: the study it presents of the making of a career by a second-generation American—in this case the son of East European Jews of modest means. Page after page of the book lays bare the incentives, drives, purposes and goals that shaped Podhoretz's life, from his earliest days in school, when a teacher of English encouraged his ambition to become a writer (in those days a poet). And it does so without depending on self-interpretation. Though the writing in *Making It* appears never less than completely frank, it seems to me that the book is most persuasive when it allows the events to speak for themselves.

A sociologically oriented critic, Podhoretz is not oblivious to the part that acculturation has played in his formation. But perhaps because he cannot remain completely objective, he often misses the most important part of this aspect of his education. His astonishment, as a Columbia undergraduate, that the question of one's success was as distasteful a subject for discussion as sex had been for the Victorians reveals how little he has probed this major American concern, even apart from its ethnic involvement. He writes:

> Most of the books I read about America assured me— and continue to do so to this day—that success was the supreme, even the only American value, and yet at Columbia College the word "successful" glided automatically into the judgment "corrupt."

Coming from an undergraduate, that observation could be taken as acute; from a critic of American literature and society, it is curiously unexamined and hollow. Granted that success is extolled as a national virtue, does it follow that society's definition of success remains constant? Can the Horatio Alger story of an era of expanding frontiers hold the same glamour and enticement in a period of consolidation and retrenchment (such as the postwar years of Podhoretz's youth clearly were)? And what about the different faces that "success" presents to the individual? As a boy, Podhoretz felt that the main thing was to be esteemed beyond this narrow circle. But he learned all too soon that the ambition to succeed involves more than the need to compensate for something one lacks. Beyond this, there was the desire for power, not only in order to impose one's will but to advance one's belief, one's total attitude. And whether one's goal was narrowly partisan (as the politician's) or boldly universal (as the artist's or scientist's), it could best be achieved if one was passionate and had hurdles to overcome.

Although Podhoretz recognizes that "the gospel of success did reign supreme" in the immigrant Jewish milieu of his childhood, he does not really see how this attitude separated him from his full-fledged American classmates, particularly those who were affluent. For them, "acceptance" or "esteem" in the sense that he means it was irrelevant; having been born to succeed, they were free to disdain the effort. Indeed, for many young people today those words hardly exist —for who needs the "acceptance" or "esteem" of a society one all but rejects? As for influence and power, the more closely you identify with your ethnic environment, the less likely you are to accept the establishment's persuasions and consequently the more readily you can plead a cause of your own. What Podhoretz describes as "the cult of failure or anti-success" is, it seems to me, simply the gap that he feels between his own strong passions and their rather pale facsimiles in the world about him.

Podhoretz makes a very cogent distinction between the obvious social climber and his own brand of blind groping toward status as a child, yet his comments reveal that he is not wholly alert to the special conditions that produced that difference. "The choice had to be blind," he says; "there was a kind of treason in it: treason toward my family, treason toward my friends." A talented child in a happy family, showered with love and admiration, he was not "alienated"; rather than admit he belonged to the "lower" class, he preferred to dismiss the whole idea of class as "a prissy triviality."

But there is something more there. The ambiguity of his position—the fact that he wants both to be a part of his environment and to improve it—rises most of all, it seems to me, from a sense of ethnic security. His is no simple "rags to riches" transformation in which an old and inferior way of life is to be replaced by a new and superior one. The second generation of a minority group with a long and rich historical past is bound to pause over those words "inferior" and "superior." The fact that, with all his ambition to become a great and famous poet, Podhoretz remained close to his family and "fiercely patriotic about Brownsville" suggests that there was some recognition by his parents (which he inevitably absorbed) that the alternative society in which they were expected to be assimilated was not necessarily morally and spiritually richer.

As Podhoretz shows, the life-style of the Jewish family that resists total assimilation is rich in ego-fulfillment. There is the traditional patronage to intellectual excellence, and there is the group response to any demonstration of it by one of its members. As the family's young genius and prizewinner, he was "quite blatantly the favorite at home."

> The adult world, and especially the female part of it, was one vast congregation of worshippers at the shrine of my diminutive godhead. They praised, they kissed, they pinched, they pulled, they hugged . . . quoting my bright sayings to one another . . . and predicted a great future for me: a doctor at the very least I would be.

Podhoretz brings up this happy aspect of his childhood to explain why he grew up knowing nothing of envy. In terms of his story, however, it may be more significant to point out how this environment helped him to fix a goal for his ambition.

In this connection it is unfortunate that Podhoretz has given so little space in his book to a person who was so instrumental in his education, namely his father. All that we learn about him is that he had been raised in an Orthodox Jewish home and was employed as a milkman for about $60 a week. But if that was all that was worth knowing about him, he would not have commanded his son's respect to the extent that he did. To please him Podhoretz not only attended Hebrew High School but also (while at Columbia) a Hebrew Seminary College. The Jewish education, as his father saw it, was to make his son not a fanatic nationalist but rather, like himself, "a tolerant Jewish survivalist . . ."

> Tolerant of any modality of Jewish existence so long as it remained identifiably and self-consciously Jewish and outraged by any species of Jewish assimilationism, whether overt or concealed. . . . The point was to be a Jew, and the way to be a Jew was to get a Jewish education, never mind about definitions, ideologies, justifications.

On the matter of religion, his father "respected observance in others and encouraged it in me," he writes, "less, I think, out of any religious convictions than out of a commitment to Jewish survival that was more instinctual than reasoned and consequently all the greater in its force."

This subtle form of parochialism did not apparently interfere with Podhoretz's academic progress at Columbia. "Utterly open, limitlessly impressionable, possessed of something like total recall," he became at once an outstanding student, collecting A + 's with such regularity that he eventually aroused hostility even among his friends, who regarded him as something of an opportunist, a Julien Sorel or a Rastignac.

But he gradually began to see through the parochialism. Studying under great teachers like Moses Hadas, Irwin Edman, Mark Van Doren and Lionel Trilling, the young undergraduate began making comparisons:

> Western culture made what the Seminary had to offer look narrow, constricted, provincial . . . less relevant to me personally than Western culture.

And while he admitted that a few of the courses were easily equal to any at Columbia, he reacted negatively to

> the strident note of apologetics and defensiveness which entered into the least detail of almost every other aspect of Seminary curriculum, the endless pep talks disguised as scholarship, the endless harping on the sufferings of the Jews; all this made my Columbia-trained sensibilities raw.

At home his sensibilities were also being wounded: "The neighborhood voices were beginning to sound coarse . . . the apartment to look tasteless and tawdry." He notes acutely: "It was my sensibilities which were being offended, and by things which had been familiar to me my whole life long." "Taste," he realizes, "is an important sociological force, capable by itself of turning strangers into brothers and brothers into strangers." The study of Western literature, more than any other force in his environment, was refining his taste and sensibilities and, by broadening his outlook, was separating him from his ethnic roots.

Had his education stopped at that point, Podhoretz's development would probably have been no different from that of most second-generation Americans: bit by bit he would have been estranged from his family and his background, retaining only a nostalgia for wisps of custom and childhood memories. But a graduate fellowship to study English at Cambridge, England, brought about some unexpected changes.

First, there was the calming effect of the class-bound society on his driving ambition; the competition hereafter would be on a higher intellectual level. He writes: "Clare [College] meant a long reprieve from being tested by others; even better, it meant reprieve from being tested by myself." Now he could ponder the values he had learned apart from their usefulness to him. And as a student of the English critic F. R. Leavis, he would learn one of the most useful lessons of his life.

Columbia had given him an overpowering taste for Western literature, and he had come to Cambridge determined to commit his life to the study of English literature. But, listening to Leavis and immersing himself in English literature, he became more and more aware of "the Englishness of English literature."

> "Western" had always meant "universal" to me, and I was for a time in some danger of jumping (as in fact others did) to the conclusion that the transcendent realm of spirit which I had once thought could be located in "culture" was actually embodied in, of all places, America. Leavis, however, inadvertently saved me from such neo-Hegelian silliness. . . . For just as life in England was teaching me what class meant as a concrete condition, studying with Leavis was opening my eyes to the particularism and historicity of literature—and, by extension, of culture in general.

He saw that while English literature produced its universal figures, it had its own "transcended parochialism . . . an occasional Keats and a multitude of Crabbes." And so he concluded:

> No more than there existed a socially neutral realm of culture in which to live, there was no such thing, I was beginning to see, as culture in the abstract; *there was only a multiplicity of cultures, each the patrimonial spiritual estate of a particular group of people,* some no doubt richer and more valuable on the whole than others, some more accessible . . . but every one of them in any case national to the core.

I have italicized a section of the above quote to emphasize the realization that eventually redirected Podhoretz on his course to fame and power. In a complex way that he analyzes only superficially, it made him decide against staying on in England and pursuing an academic career.

But if he rejected the world that Cambridge opened up to him, where would he look for an alternative? The Trillings, whom he had come to know socially, candidly pointed out to him that it was pretty impossible in America to become a critic outside the academy. But, said Mrs. Trilling, there were other things in the world to do—and she suggested law as a career. Though Podhoretz was "outraged and humiliated" by the suggestion, it set him thinking. If he could not be an *academic* critic, he could be a critic nonetheless. When *Commentary* came to him with an offer to write for it, he saw where his opportunity lay.

Founded right after World War II by the American Jewish Committee, *Commentary* was not a literary magazine but a journal of opinion primarily set up to examine problems of Jewish concern. Under the editorship of the erudite Elliott Cohen, it had departed sufficiently from parochial concerns to deserve the description of "a kind of Jewish *Harper's*"; but it was more scholarly than *Harper's,* and it aimed to popularize at a higher level. In Podhoretz's words, it had attracted "intellectuals to whom the idea had never occurred that things Jewish could be talked about with the same disinterestedness, the same candor, the same range of reference and the same resonances as any serious subject." In the period of ten years its staff of contributors would become interchangeable with that of *Partisan Review:* leading critics, intellectuals and opinion-makers (who would become known as the New York Literary Establishment), all involved in a running criticism of American life and culture, all writing in a hypercritical, learned, elusive style. They came to represent "the family"—the Jewish family (since so many of them had Jewish ancestry), spanning two generations.

Podhoretz, who early in the 1950s had become established as an up-and-coming young critic writing not only for *Commentary* but for *Partisan Review* and even the *New Yorker,* gravitated toward his literary family with the ingenuous delight of a youngster going to one bang-up party after another. Their parties (at which all the critics referred to one another by first name) made him, in fact, starry-eyed. But more than that, he writes, "it was the attention of the family I most dreamed of arousing. There was no doubt in my mind that it was *my* family, for reading its writing was like hearing a call from the depths of my very soul."

Half estranged from his own family after Cambridge, and suffering a loss of center after two years of service in the army, Podhoretz got much the same kind of ego-fulfillment from his association with this new family as he once had derived from his life in Brownsville. Only now he would find his self-identity on the level where it would matter—the intellectual level.

There is no need here to report in detail on the stages of his progress from editorial assistant on the magazine to the editorship in 1960. It must be said that the fierce drive that made him triumph over the restrictions imposed on him by the magazine's policy and its policyholders does not always put him in the most favorable light. The urge to power never does. And he has the candor to tell us that power was what he sought. But not hierarchical power (the Army kind). What he wanted was "power to put autonomy to a truly creative use." And he had every chance of succeeding.

For, while he absorbed the method and the style of "the family," his philosophical attitude diverged rather sharply from theirs. So prevalent was the attitude of alienation in the second-generation writers of the early 1950s that a renegade of "the family"—Saul Bellow—could write a novel (*The Adventures of Augie March*) arguing against an attitude of withdrawal. Podhoretz's highly critical review of the novel revealed his own radical departure from this attitude at the same time that it criticized the forced and unnatural form that Bellow's affirmation took. Having himself tackled the problem of literary pluralism, Podhoretz had come to a different conclusion from Bellow. Like Bellow he rejected the view of Jewish life as exotica. But it did not mean that one could overnight become a fullfledged American writer with an "American" point of view:

Writing was hard enough, but to have to write with only that part of one's being which had been formed by the acculturation-minded public schools and by the blindly ethnicized English departments of the colleges was like being asked to compete in a race with the leg cut off at the thigh.

Bellow might fool himself into thinking that the world rejected you because you rejected the world. Podhoretz knew better. It was a question of whether the world would *accept* you.

This indeed became the crux of what *Commentary* could achieve, and it became Podhoretz's ambition to make the magazine reflect this view. When he was offered the editorship of the magazine, he made sure it was understood that he would hold Jewish material of a parochial kind to a minimum, but at the same time he would establish for the Jewish view an intellectual modus vivendi that would not be a phony form of Americanism.

It is interesting to read what he has to say on this subject:

Each person was a composite of extrinsic identities—regional, religious, ethnic, occupational—every one of which played a determining role in his fate greater than his own merits alone could possibly play.

And, he continues, the individual's progress was limited by "the status of the particularistic communities from which he came," that status being determined eventually by a "neutral territory," allegedly devoid of any ethnic particularism—which the mass media represented.

Under Podhoretz's direction *Commentary*'s circulation increased from 20,000 to 60,000. In all modesty, for the first time, Podhoretz lays this success at the door of a sudden change in American taste. "Jews," he remarks, "were culturally all the rage in America . . . they were replacing the Southern writers." The fact that *Commentary*'s views were respected nationally was made evident by President Johnson's invitation to him, along with six other intellectuals, to advise him on "things I would like to see him do." Podhoretz writes:

> I never had so much trouble writing anything. As an intellectual I was as ghettoized as my ancestors in Eastern Europe had been as Jews. It was not I (nor they) who had built the ghetto, but it would take more than a mere tearing down of the walls to get me out of it.

He couldn't really tell the president what to do, because he had never thought it possible that the country could be shaped in accordance with his ideas.

Now, as editor of a leading intellectual magazine, he had achieved this power. And this is Podhoretz's real triumph, which he fails to see; a triumph his more passive Columbia classmates could not know. He had helped impose his ideas; he had helped (along with other writers of his generation) to make Jewish writers and their concerns less remote from American life. He had, as an editor of *Commentary,* helped, in fact, alter the "neutral" territory so that it would prove increasingly less difficult or embarrassing for ethnic groups to cross it.

1968

Spearhead
of British Modernism

The *Bloomsbury Group* by J. K. Johnstone has the intrinsic merit of all studies which break ground. We have had many individual studies of the writers and artists who comprised the British spearhead of the modernist movement, but of the group as a whole, aside from D. S. Mirsky's *The Intelligentsia of Great Britain* (which was too damaging to count as criticism), we have had only fragments that have played up the personalities in the cast.

Mr. Johnstone is not impervious to the charm and color of that diverse group which combined, among others, the talents of biographer Lytton Strachey, art critic Roger Fry, novelists Virginia Woolf and E. M. Forster, socialist historian Leonard Woolf, and economist John Maynard Keynes. Vividly but briefly, he sets the stage of those inspired meetings held in the sedate Victorian atmosphere of the late Sir Leslie Stephen's home—with shy young Virginia Stephen (the future Mrs. Woolf) absorbing alike the gay and serious talk of her brothers' Cambridge friends. But he deliberately avoids the anecdotal approach to give us the sterner stuff of criticism: exposition, interpretation and synthesis.

Only perspective can bring validity to literary judgments. Mr. Johnstone achieves perspective when he places Bloomsbury midway between Victorian and modern values. The Group's impassioned faith in art, too often identified with an effete bohemianism, is at last revealed for what it was: the vigorous beginning of a new tradition in literature which (to paraphrase Mr. Johnstone) aimed at making art moral while at the same time freeing it from morals. This was not, strictly speaking, "art for art's sake." Though aesthetics for these young intellectuals became more important than conventions and propriety, its pursuit had much more than pleasure as its aim. What they sought through art was a heightened awareness of life that would make moral responsibility instinctive and natural. If beauty led the way to truth, sincerity in human relationships was the criterion of both.

Mr. Johnstone is at pains to show us how the three separate influences that created Bloomsbury were connected. The first of these he sees as deriving from the ideal of friendship that Keynes and Strachey, to mention only two, transmitted to Bloomsbury as former members of the elite undergraduate society at Cambridge known as the Apostles. The belief that only in an atmosphere of relaxed intimacy could the truth be successfully pursued became Bloomsbury's creed even before it had felt the influence of G. E. Moore's *Principia Ethica*. Moore's new ethics, with its emphasis on the affinity between feeling and thought, seemed ready made for this close-knit group. They were in tune with other aspects of Moore's philosophy: his repudiation of the utilitarian function of good, his identification of the good with the beautiful. They saw, in his insistence on intrinsic values, a radical departure from Victorian standards of morality, though not from morality itself.

When Moore wrote: "By far the most valuable things . . . are certain states of consciousness, which may be roughly described as the pleasures of human intercourse and the enjoyment of beautiful objects. . . . It is only for the sake of these things that anyone can be justified in performing any public or private duty," he was at the same time strengthening the Apostles' belief in the value of friendship and paving the way for the third important influence, Roger Fry's creed of art.

It was Fry who, by examining the structure of art, finally traced a systematic relationship between beauty and truth (the latter being synonymous with the highest good). Mr. Johnstone's analytical approach suggests, in a way that Virginia Woolf's biographical one could not, the extent of the art critic's impact on the new literature. If Mr. Johnstone underestimates Henry James's earlier contribution to the art of fiction, he leaves little doubt in our minds that it is to Fry we owe our most advanced concept of the novel as an "autonomous" work of art—and by "work of art" Fry meant something "completely self-consistent, self-supporting and self-contained," detached from the values and demands of ordinary, "instinctive" life. The author follows with contagious persistence the course of Fry's reasoning from the initial premise that "real art is concerned with the contemplation of formal relations" to his final summation of the artist as one who seeks *emotional* harmonies with the same intensity and purpose as the scientist seeks *causal* harmonies, the aim of both being a deeper understanding of reality.

It remains for Mr. Johnstone to show—through the interpretation of particular works—the artistic validity of Bloomsbury's teachings. This becomes by far the more challenging portion of the study, for at least two of the three writers he has chosen to examine closely make the highest demand of aesthetic appreciation. In the one hundred pages on Forster and the fifty each on Strachey and Virginia Woolf, his stated intention is to analyze their works in terms of their composition. Actually, he does little more on this score than labor the point that they are well-constructed "wholes." But, then, you want to say, structure has always been important to good fiction. The novelty was not Bloomsbury's preoccupation with form but, as suggested earlier, the new concept of form which it evolved.

When faced with the work of art itself—with *A Passage to India* or *To the Lighthouse* or *Eminent Victorians*—Mr. Johnstone becomes generally a less exacting critic. Although he gives us fresh insights into Forster's world, with its focus on human relationships, its faith in "the aristocracy of the sensitive, the considerate, the plucky," he never quite conveys the particular *quality* of Forster's prose. With Strachey he is less distracted by "content," but, while he demonstrates that the biographies employed the selectivity and organic unity of art, we are not persuaded that the result in each instance was art.

The final chapter on Virginia Woolf, though the best of the three, draws attention to one other weakness of this generally important work. With her rare gift for transforming feeling into form and her superior grasp of the logic of the emotions, Mrs. Woolf was Bloomsbury incarnate. Quoting extensively from her essays, Mr. Johnstone does not fail to indicate the many points on which she agreed with Fry. But, though he implies it, he does not substantially make the point that in the end she transcended Bloomsbury, seeking in the artist's vision not simply a pathway to reality but an expansion of it. Only a more comprehensive view would have allowed Mr. Johnstone to admit this, and to admit along with that fact the ultimate impact of modern values on Bloomsbury and particularly on Forster and Mrs. Woolf. This does not, however, diminish the book's considerable achievement as the first objective analysis of Bloomsbury philosophy and of the literature it nurtured.

1954

A Passion
for Letters:
Scofield Thayer
and the Dial

A literary quiz on the 1920s might consider the following questions: (1) What well-known American woman poet set aside her writing in mid-career to edit a literary magazine for three years? (2) Who or what was "Bel Esprit"? (3) Describe John Quinn's relationship to the writers of the twenties. (4) Name the editor described below:

"Slender of build, swift of movement, strikingly pale, with coal-black hair, black eyes veiled and flashing, lips curved like those of Byron, he seemed to many the embodiment of the aesthete. . . . This was far from the case. Art and letters he pursued but with a purpose so elevated and so impassioned that he remained insulated from the ironical comments about him. He administered his wealth largely as a trust, supporting or helping to support many young writers and artists."

If the answers* are not immediately forthcoming, it is not because the questions are esoteric but because they concern personalities in a period which (unlike our own) took less interest in the writer than in his writing. And if the facts in themselves seem tangential, within the context of Nicholas Joost's *Scofield Thayer and the Dial* they become significant. Together with many more such facts, they have produced a book that is as absorbing as a Le Carré thriller and much more enlightening than many a gossip-ography currently cluttering the bookstands.

Joost's book, though a slapdash job in some respects (it is long-winded, unfocused and at times needlessly imprecise), is an impressive example of imaginative publishing too rarely encountered these days when books are published with preconceived notions of what readers want and need. No one at Southern Illinois University Press was apparently stopped by such considerations, and wisely. For the reader himself could not have guessed how deeply his interest would be engaged. So infectious is Joost's enthusiasm for his subject—the parallel histories of a magazine and a literary era—that the most banal facts take on importance.

In his pages the *Dial* is palpably alive—not a relic of the days of Emerson (the original *Dial* dates from 1840) nor even the faded dusty-rose item tucked alongside the "classics" of our parents' day. We see it as it was in its heyday, an organ of communication as vital as any we display on our coffee tables. Yet not *really* like any other. The *Dial*, as Scofield Thayer and his partner, Dr. James Sibley Watson, Jr., fashioned it, resembled nothing that had ever come before or has come since.

Thayer, whose word portrait by Alyse Gregory is quoted above, was a young Harvard and Oxford man of cultivated tastes, with

---

*1. Marianne Moore served as managing editor of the *Dial* from 1926 to 1929. 2. Ezra Pound's name for his money-raising scheme (which never materialized) to help support T. S. Eliot and other needy, deserving writers. 3. Today little more than a name, John Quinn, a lawyer and art patron, was an impressive presence and benefactor. 4. Scofield Thayer of the *Dial*.

mildly radical ideas and substantial wealth. When he acquired the *Dial* in 1920, that fortnightly magazine was "hanging on a shoestring," though its previous publisher, Martyn Johnson, had enlisted such "names" as Thorsten Veblen, George Moore, John Dewey and Randolph Bourne. Thayer, whose interests ran counter to the prevailing concern with politics and social questions, was even less inclined to concede to mass appeal. A monthly magazine of new literature and art (predominantly critical), with no political, regional or academic ties, the new *Dial* was an audacious venture such as no foundation today would risk. Yet Thayer's *Dial* survived for nine years, paradoxically increasing its readership in number while limiting it in kind. In Joost's words, "the editors honestly believed that the publication of fine creative and critical work was an enterprise in civilization that would do something to stir America from the apathy of imagination that had fallen on it."

Whatever Thayer's and Watson's avowed aims, the *Dial* from 1920 to 1929 proved (contrary to our current cynicism) that literary taste can be directed and ultimately improved. Needless to say, it was Thayer's good fortune that the contemporary art he championed was naturally irresistible.

Balancing new and familiar names in both European and American writing, juxtaposing the mildly avant-garde in style with the more traditional, the *Dial* achieved in each issue a cornucopia of elegant, penetrating, witty, adventurous and, above all, aesthetically satisfying writing. It is hard to imagine a current publication with an equivalent mixture of T. S. Eliot and Ezra Pound, e. e. cummings and Marianne Moore, D. H. Lawrence and Dos Passos, Thomas Mann and Yeats, Ortega y Gasset and Santayana, Bertrand Russell and Anatole France. (And the list goes on and on.) Similarly, in its art section, it would be hard to match such an assemblage as Picasso and Brancusi, Renoir and Braque, Kokoschka and Bonnard. (And that list, too, stretches.)

How could the *Dial* do it? What was the magic that made its idealism pay off, in terms of circulation—a significant jump from 3,000 to 22,000? One answer, of course, is that it had money to lose—sometimes as much as $50,000 in one year. Another answer lies in the prestige it represented. The year in which it published Eliot's *The Waste Land* (1922) the magazine's sales doubled. But beyond these, the magazine's success hinged on a fortuitous set of circumstances.

The avant-garde writing of the day had not only superior literary quality but a broad humanistic base that counterbalanced much of the difficulty of the new aesthetics. If modernism at its best was more palatable than much contemporary writing is today, it might be argued that, at its source, it was much less radical; if traditions were attacked, if the new psychology, the new ethics sought to discredit the past, it never precluded the possibility of *new* utopias.

A magazine like the *Dial* had much to gain, too, by the fact that specialization had not yet destroyed the possibility of a combination of the arts. A Santayana could write on Freud, an Eliot on Stravinsky, and critics like Edmund Wilson and Malcolm Cowley could direct their criticisms to readers whose interests were as diverse as their own. Whether or not a relationship existed between the growing national consciousness of the period and the flowering of American poetry in the second and third decades of the century, it is possible that a certain sense of wonder about who we are and where we were going played a part in the abundance of poetic expression.

This same feeling of confidence in our separateness (bluntly expressed by the magazine's art critic, Henry McBride: "I think the time has come when it is no longer necessary for the first-rate American to go to Paris") must have made it possible for the *Dial* to admit European writing in such profusion into its pages. Only artists confident in their own strength will let the door open to outside influence. The interchange of American and European letters in the *Dial* would ultimately leave its impact on both American readers and writers.

In all fairness to Joost's book, these speculations are never stated abstractly but only implied in the course of his minutely traced account. These are afterthoughts. As we read, we are fascinated by the facts, particularly those which add human dimension to the story. If so much of the material is fresh after so much shedding of print on the twenties, it is because writers of that time had not yet become celebrities whose every idiosyncrasy was exploited for mass consumption. Except for Hemingway and Fitzgerald (whose lives had direct bearing on their works), it was the work, not the man, that mattered. The *Dial*, with its high regard for aesthetics, respected that view more than any other publication, despite the temptation which its relations with so many prominent writers of the day must have presented.

Joost himself has also avoided the temptation to indulge in the kind of gossip that has filled so many memoirs of those years. Instead he has sought out the incidents, the events that illuminate. The involved story of the *Dial's* purchase of *The Waste Land* and of the poem's winning the coveted Dial Award is interesting not only for what it reveals about the poet's ability to drive a bargain (one really his due) but for what it suggests of the quality of the relationship that existed between editors and writers. Similarly, what we learn about Pound's role in promoting the careers of his contemporaries should help raise our estimate of that poet's service to letters.

As for Thayer, his portrait unfortunately is still incomplete. Joost hardly enters into his personal life—whether because it is irrelevant to his story or simply because it is not yet for release, we are not told. But Thayer's personal characteristics are not to be missed: his perfectionism as an editor (he would redo a whole issue for one error!), his strongly held opinions, his footloose habit of disappearing from the scene at intervals (which necessitated strong staff support), his determination to get his way, though never at the risk of losing a major talent for his magazine. Thayer was not the most infallible of editors (he rejected Hemingway, was unduly severe on O'Neill, said he "detested" modern art—on the last he had the good judgment to defer to Watson's views). But what he had in large measure was a passion for letters. Taste combined with means and a sense of responsibility was the passport to his unique success. Would that we had a few Thayers today!

1965

A Specialist
of the Hoax:
Max Beerbohm

He had flair (some called it impudence), an inventive imagination, and that rarest of comic gifts—mimicry. Still in his
early twenties in the waning years of the last century, he was
a presence, a force to contend with: "the incomparable Max," G. B.
Shaw called him, baffled by his versatility; couching his envy, Lytton
Strachey classified him as "the smallest genius in the world," while
Oscar Wilde announced that the gods had bestowed on young Max
"the gift of perpetual old age." Max was, of course, Max Beerbohm,
who knew and parodied all the literary greats of his day, drawing
blood even as he charmed and entertained—and epitomized his age.

Though he became the legendary figure supreme among the
English "decadents," no one so far has identified him with a "secret
life" of vice or neurosis. It is unlikely that anyone ever will. The so-
called intimate memoir by S. N. Behrman of a decade ago dealt only
with reminiscences of the writer-artist in Rapallo, Italy, where he had
gone into temporary retirement after two strenuous decades in London as man about town. His bright personality, on the other hand, has
diverted attention from the special features of his talent. A full cen-

tury after his birth, in a delightfully illustrated commemorative volume *The Lies of Art,* John Felstiner sets the biographical dimension aside to look into "the inner frame of his art." Giving us a critical basis for an appreciation of Beerbohm, he also confirms, if only obliquely, the suspicion Max's fans have had that he is "our contemporary."

Initially, it is the "eccentric" of the eighteen nineties who holds the stage. As Mr. Felstiner wisely acknowledges at the start, Beerbohm had to be part of his age before he could step outside to criticize it. In the development of his art, nothing was more intrinsic than his complete identification, while still at Oxford, with the stance of dandyism. A true disciple of Wilde via Baudelaire and Pater, he looked on the clothes-consciousness and fastidiousness of the dandy as manifestations of a philosophy of art that saw artifice as superior to nature because it could improve on man. His first essay for the *Yellow Book,* "A Defence of Cosmetics," was shocking in his day. It was a more playful version of Wilde's "The Decay of Lying" and Baudelaire's "Praise of Makeup," but like them it established a need for "the lies of art," for the artist's mask as a technique combining form with subject. Resisting the Victorians' "monstrous worship of facts," Beerbohm, Mr. Felstiner says, "fell into what might be called an aesthetic heresy of individualism; that being, not doing, is the aim of life; that one should look and also live like a work of art."

But the heresy—and particularly the cultivation of hedonism into which dandyism lapsed—did not settle permanently with Max. A working journalist and gregarious half-brother of the actor Sir Herbert Beerbohm-Tree, he increasingly turned away from himself toward the world. What he retained of the lessons of the masters was the aesthetic essence: the importance of the mask, of illusion, as a source of truth. Upon a voluminous flow of essays, stories, fables and caricatures (many of himself in top hat, with large, sad, childlike eyes) which he contributed to *Savoy, Punch* and some forty other journals and newspapers, he affixed the distinctive Beerbohm signature. Always ironically attuned to the bogus aspects of his epoch, he made new fictions out of dull realities.

A Specialist of the Hoax: Max Beerbohm

He was a specialist of the hoax—fake historical figures and made-up literary references appear throughout his work. His most famous hoax, "A Peep into the Past," is a fabricated interview with Wilde that strips the corpulent hedonist of the last shred of his human and artistic dignity; mercifully, it remained unpublished in Wilde's lifetime. His book-length work, *Seven Men,* dealing with fictitious late Victorian and Edwardian characters as if they actually existed, anticipates the sardonic fantasies of Nabokov and Borges.

Equally gifted with words and lines, Beerbohm was more facile with the latter, drawing his best after he had made a visit to his club. Unlike the "decadent" Beardsley, who embellished reality to provoke a perverse response, Beerbohm merely simplified what he saw, exaggerating a single feature to draw out a hidden flaw. From the simpler political and social cartoons, he moved on to the more sophisticated literary caricatures in which he anatomized not only the figures or features of Kipling, Henry James, Wells or the Rossettis, among others, but the cultural concepts or cults they represented.

Mr. Felstiner is perhaps not discriminating enough in his estimate of Beerbohm's prose style. Many of the early essays are marred for modern readers by their elaborate rococo manner. In retrospect, his drama criticism is narrow and biased, and his fantastic Oxford romance, "Zuleika Dobson," is actually readable only in parts. Max is best, and closest to us, when he exercises his sharp critical mind. He is consistently successful when he imitates, with subtle ironic effects, the diverse styles of Conrad, Dickens, Bennett, James and Galsworthy; and when he mimics the vague, whimsical manner of George Moore and Pater as art critics, he not only amuses but also "rebuilds a whole structure connecting actuality, art and criticism."

It was Beerbohm's good fortune to choose as subjects for his parodies writers and artists whose features would not fade with time. His long career—he died in 1956, having been knighted two decades earlier—was assured by the fact that he had initially identified with the persons he ridiculed and was thus able to see them in depth. Though Mr. Felstiner's study is somewhat lean in its peripheral references, it gives us the most thoroughly interpretive portrait of the artist we have yet had. Max the man is only implied, at times most provocatively (as in his growing vindictiveness toward Wilde). In the end he was not the true aesthete. Beyond "the lies of art" he advocated, he never ceased to grope toward a *reasonable* truth.

1972

Black Odyssey, White World

"**O** *saisons, o châteaux!/ Quelle âme est sans défauts?*" ("O seasons, O castles!/ What soul is without blemishes?") wrote Arthur Rimbaud, creating the mystique of the poet's "season in hell" en route to an ultimate vision of the world. Unlike Odysseus, who enlarged his experience through a variety of scenes and human contacts, the poet on his inward journey pursues a hidden kernel in himself that will transform experience at the moment he perceives it. It is a hard and lonely discipline that presupposes a certain social indifference and freedom from mundane concerns.

Though Vincent O. Carter was a black writer without independent means and unrelentingly hounded by his demon (actual and imagined racial prejudice), he started on a similar "voyage of the mind" nearly a century later, thousands of miles away from his native Kansas City. Settling somewhat accidentally in the capital of Switzerland, he turned from the need to become a "visible," respected member of society to the still deeper need to join the "human race" by subordinating his individual and racial self. Without the magic of Rimbaud's language, Carter can only fitfully convey his own exalted sense of what the French poet called "I is another."

But the record of his unique self-exile is, in sum, so awesome and gripping that it is hard to believe it took sixteen years for it to get published. According to Herbert R. Lottman's informative preface, *The Bern Book* nearly did not get published at all—because it did not fall into a distinct literary category. Essentially autobiographical, its narrative is interspersed with brief discourses on Bern, on art, on places and people, all held together by poetic apostrophes that evoke the landscape of a tortured psyche. Though on occasion he can match Richard Wright's inner rage and graphic writing, Carter's anger remains muted. "I write," he confesses, "in order to empty my form of its content so that I can stop dying and live once and for all."

Wright, who also used literature as a means of personal survival, once wrote that black men are not emotionally independent enough to face "the naked experience" of their lives. There is classic proportion in Carter's defiance of this view. Leaving the bourgeois comforts of his home in America, he dares to expose himself to countries where the black man is such a rarity as to be thought an anomaly. With $3,000 in traveler's checks in his pocket, a mind filled with the writings of French poets and philosophers, and an inborn craving for the "unknown," Carter first settles in Paris, where he endures squalor and suspicion. Paris after the war is not the Paris he has known as a serviceman, and the covert insults he suffers obliterate his romantic feelings for the city.

He moves on to Munich, to Amsterdam (where he feels even less at home), and he finally finds friends in Bern—that "clean, polished, shipshape city." There his "complexes" (as friends call them) grow. Doors slam in his face, knives and forks drop from plates, heads turn and babies cry when he approaches. He does not need to know the words to recognize "the language of scorn and ridicule." When people ask him personal questions, Carter feels they are "probing into the most intimate parts of his consciousness with their dirty fingers." "I am not a freak," he protests to a group of frightened children he wants to befriend.

Yet he stays on, the sensuous, outgoing, curious side of his nature responding to slightly patronizing dinner invitations, chance encounters in cafés and tearooms, and casual affairs with willing barmaids. In cramped quarters, with eviction always a threat, he fills his notebooks, remembering that "Poe had waited. Faulkner had waited." Though his stories are rejected, other doors open. Radio Bern invites him to give his impressions of the city. His hopes no sooner soar than they are dashed by the realization that he is expected to project a stereotyped image of the American Negro as a contented, spirituals-singing creature. Instead of stirring up his social consciousness, the experience only intensifies his penchant for self-probing. A new dimension of freedom is now revealed to him. He remembers the spider he has watched on the Kirchenfeld bridge, its unconscious goal so completely equal to its conscious movements. Since "the Will is Free only if man adheres to his form," he must accept "the most terrible thing of all, to face myself."

Eventually Carter becomes a "migrant mendicant," living mainly on the charity of friends (who have ceased being "patronizing"). Though he now has a certain status as a writer and is called "Herr Carter," there are times when he perversely exults in being "a black nigger," completely himself, "like a tree, a rock, a spider or an Englishman." His wariness relaxed, he makes analogies between the way the black man feels in a white society and the way the Swiss feel in the presence of the Germans. He is comforted to think that the Swiss are, after all, "just like me."

Now the real voyage begins. He feels himself becoming "myriad particles of perception," partaking of "the nature of All Things." He develops an ironic humor and experiences alternating periods of clarity and confusion. When he is rational, distinctions between "You and I," "Good and Bad" tighten. But in his "disembodied," "sublime" state, he returns to the spider image: "sensing that all was just as it was, as it is, as it will be, because all *is*." The mystical vision is fleeting. In his desire to control and "improve" himself, Carter continues to cling to the actual world. And the nature of his "voyage" changes to accommodate him.

Carter's prose is most vivid when he hews close to an object, a scene—a spider, a bridge, the silence of the town at midnight are evocatively rendered. His imagination, verging on the hallucinatory, responds best to momentary reactions. I would love to read his still unpublished "Faulknerian" novel just to see if the "voyage" he started still sustains him. On the evidence in this book, I suspect he is more Odysseus than Rimbaud, needing a firm worldly anchor for the self he finds so hard to lose.

1973

Britain's
Lopsided View

The reputation of the *Times Literary Supplement* is unequaled in the world. That enduring and timeless British publication is the supreme standard by which all literary journalism is measured, particularly in America, where awareness of the high seriousness of literature is of relatively recent origin. Indeed the *TLS* has been a kind of thorn in the side of the larger American literary supplements, making them aspire at times to an unreasonably lofty level and, failing at this, drawing to themselves criticism that is essentially unjustified. What these super-critics fail to see is that the *TLS* is a unique British phenomenon, a cultural institution as fixed and autonomous as its ancient universities. Just as no Oxford or Cambridge don could conceivably break through the conventional academic mold, so no single British author or artist can hope to filter through the dense anonymous façade of the *TLS* to herald a new dawn.* A towering mound of tradition—like eternity itself—lies in wait, diminishing the reality of the moment, affixing all things to their proper place in the scale.

Since this article was published, the TLS has changed its policy of anonymous reviewing, and all its reviewers are now identified.

Like all British institutions, the *TLS* has felt the pressures of the new era and one of its boldest gestures toward it has been a relaxing of characteristic British resistance to American culture. In a society which is beginning to admit the culture of the working class, it is no longer possible to continue the myth of the raw, the uncouth, the mercenary American. The very traits once held against us are now seen as worthy of being emulated. America is now equated with vigor, freshness and originality and is earning respect for achieving a successful mass culture. In 1958, in a massive special issue titled "The American Imagination," the *TLS* sang a paean of praise to America that was tantamount to admission into the "Commonwealth of Cultured Nations." It told the world that we had "arrived."

In the fall of 1960, directing the same close scrutiny upon Britain itself, in a sequel called "The British Imagination," the *TLS* proceeds with much greater caution. The newness, the vitality it admired in the American arts, in England are given a heavy-handed evaluation. They cannot exist for themselves, merely to give pleasure, but must have a "national" or "social" purpose. For just as it appeared to have discovered America last year, so this year the *TLS* has discovered an England that is in the throes of social revolution. The editorial writer speaks of "the consciousness of having grown and changed in the most alarming and unexpected way." He adds, ingenuously: "We tend to be ignorant of the deepest revolutions in our own lives until chance in the form of a stranger's remark jolts us into an awareness of them."

The "jolt," the sudden impact, is overwhelming. In contrast to the promise of tomorrow, the bright vistas of yesteryear now appear dull and dim. A carping, self-deflating tone dominates nearly all the articles, particularly when the achievements of the recent past are discussed. For once, poise, perspective, sense of balance are thrown to the wind.

British autobiography, however entertaining, has never, it is maintained, been really interested in the analysis of ideas: the British have no Julian Bendas, nor "even an effective Alfred Kazin." Instead:

"Our memories are cluttered with nannies, teas under the limes, the sound of bat on ball and witty Oxford conversation."

By current *TLS* standards, postwar Britain has produced only four novelists worth bothering about: C. P. Snow, Anthony Powell, Angus Wilson and Graham Greene. (There's a condescending reference to Kingsley Amis as a comic writer.) But good as these are, they are not Saul Bellow (creator of that four-star model of American vitality, Augie March). "Our novelists have been conspicuously reticent in showing their characters at work," the article writer complains, and by work he means *work*. British writers just aren't in touch: Elizabeth Bowen, P. H. Newby, Ivy Compton-Burnett do not tell us of "the problems of our time"; they are "too narrowly literary." Only Wilson and Greene are seen as presenting "a realistic picture of the world we live in." And not only does the English novel lack a Saul Bellow to give it "life," "the sad truth is that we have no women writers comparable in wit and intelligence to Miss Mary McCarthy or in real sensibility to Carson McCullers."

It is only in its comic vision that the modern English novel is deemed superior, and this because it serves a social and moral purpose. Again the kudos go to Angus Wilson and Anthony Powell (no mention of Iris Murdoch, John Braine, Keith Waterhouse, etc.). Here the Americans are brought down a peg or two. For while English comic writers always made a social point, the humor of a James Thurber or an S. J. Perelman is best characterized as "pure." (Crossing the Atlantic must "purify" humorous writers.) Iris Murdoch (has no one heard of her?) seems to us a "purer" comic writer than either of these American writers, as does Joyce Cary (also curiously ignored).

There are other confusions. While British music and ballet are extolled for becoming more "national," English poetry is charged with being "aggressively British," insular and regional in tone, the model today being Robert Graves of the "modest, good poem" rather than the cosmopolite T. S. Eliot or Ezra Pound. This article consists mainly of paraphrased opinions of a visiting American poet-critic, and it somehow manages to lump together William Plomer, John Betjeman, Edwin Muir and Philip Larkin.

A related essay begins by berating the English for becoming increasingly insensitive to their language, for cultivating an anti-style so widespread that it threatens to break through social barriers. But the situation has its brighter side where the British imagination is concerned. A new realism has hit the theater of the East End, and by juxtaposing the nonliterary language of Shelagh Delaney and Arnold Wesker to that of Joel Chandler Harris, Mark Twain and Ernest Hemingway, the *TLS* writer makes it all sound very respectable and valid. (Americans to the rescue again!)

An inferiority complex before the U.S. in the areas of education and science appears more justified. There is poignance in the writer's bald statement that "Britain is the poor relation in the U.K.-U.S.-U.S.S.R. triangle." The British imagination in science, for one, is evidently hampered by economics.

But lest it appear to be overpessimistic and out of line with "the raw, new ideas stirring contemporary England," the *TLS* also does some judicious yea-saying. It approves of the "practical criticism" of F. R. Leavis and Richard Hoggart, who see literature as a moral concern: "the criticism of a society strenuously responding to what threatens its health." For much the same "health" reasons, one suspects, it champions the new attitude toward poetry as "a gesture of response to life," and as "a socially cooperative activity." It not only favors the new movies which, unlike the novels, picture the working classes as persons, but suggests that they are superior to the purely artistic ones of the recent past. (Does no one remember *Kind Hearts and Coronets, Brief Encounter, The Fallen Idol,* etc., etc.?)

The *TLS* also sees a future for the British imagination in television and radio, where the shining light these days is the playwright Harold Pinter of *The Caretaker* fame. It even sees scope for the imagination in jazz which is characterized as "a manifestation of class feeling . . . a democratic revolt in the field of culture." And it feels encouraged by the recent tendency in ballet toward a more national choreography that emphasizes narrative and folk tradition. Presumably this will turn an "aristocratic" medium into a "democratic" one. But will the result be more imaginative?

The most striking demonstration of confusion between artistic values and utilitarian ends appears in the articles on British music (almost solely restricted to Vaughan Williams and Benjamin Britten), British sculpture and architecture. It is here that the need rises to defend subsidized art: "As the Middle Ages proved so well, a reasonable amount of talent can always be found and made by training and by the prospect of a living afterwards." It is not on the grounds of imagination but of art in the service of society that the impersonal style of contemporary British architecture is justified.

Defining a national imagination is a task that calls for imagination. A mere sampling of these articles, with their heavy, tiresomely repetitious, impersonal style will suggest that imagination is not one of the *TLS*'s stronger features. But the initial error, perhaps, was in conceiving a British imagination without its Irish, Scotch and Welsh components. It is from this mixture that British culture derives its marvelous variety, its flexibility, its breadth and depth. I do not mean that the *TLS* should have carried separate articles on the contributions of these groups—that is something too intangible. But some concrete evidence should have been given of the effect this threefold heritage has had on the Anglo-Saxon imagination. Without it, there could not have been that incredible conglomeration of practicalness and idealism, common sense and fantasy, earthiness and lyric vision, tradition and experiment that is the sum total of the British imagination.

Undeniably Britain is H. G. Wells, George Orwell and C. P. Snow, but it is *also* William Blake and John Donne and Dylan Thomas; it is James Joyce and Virginia Woolf and E. M. Forster; it is Lewis Carroll and Walter de la Mare. The influences of this diverse latter group have not, thank heaven, completely vanished yet, though it appears to suit the purpose of the *TLS* at the moment not to recognize or even to remember them.

1961

Despiritualized Americans: Soviet Views of American Literature

My first acquaintance with Marxist criticism was through the work of the eminent Hungarian critic György Lukács, who practiced Socialist Realism in modified form. A work like his *Studies in European Realism* (English translation 1950) is eye-opening to anyone whose orientation to the works of Balzac, Tolstoy and other nineteenth-century giants of fiction has been wholly literary and aesthetic. In his study of Balzac, for example, Lukács uncovered the authentic art of a writer fully aware of the socio-historical sources of his fiction. Discounting the book's ideological overtones, one gleans from its vantage point not only new insights into Balzac but also the very concept of "great realism."

But the literary sensibility of a Lukács is not a common commodity, and Soviet criticism today appears to have profited little from his example. This conclusion is inevitable after a reading of Carl Proffer's immensely valuable (though not always smoothly translated) anthology containing pieces from Soviet publications of the last decade titled *Soviet Criticism of American Literature in the Sixties.* What makes the volume particularly useful and interesting is that the criticism is devoted solely to recent American fiction; thus, along with what it tells us about the state of criticism in that still elusive land, it exposes what the critic in Soviet Russia thinks about America and her literature.

Heaven knows, American life is not utopian—but in the minds of Soviet critics it is beyond redemption. The best of them, writing in *Foreign Literature, The Literary Gazette* and massive volumes like *Problems of 20th Century American Literature* (1970), have reached this verdict from a reading of modern American novelists such as Faulkner, Hemingway, Fitzgerald, McCullers, Updike, Mailer, Bellow, Salinger, Styron and Cheever—nearly all translated for the first time in the nineteen sixties. Though generally praised for their "openness to reality" and their "moral impulses," these novelists are seen as betrayers of the "despiritualized mass consumer society," and in some instances (i.e., Fitzgerald) as victims of capitalist "dehumanization."

With scarcely a reference to an American writer before 1920 (*Moby Dick,* we learn, was translated for the first time in 1961), and none at all to best-selling works that more nearly represent public taste, these critics presume to generalize about America from a literal and random reading of some of our most sophisticated writers. Apart from the limitations imposed by a vocabulary studded with hackneyed phrases (a word repeatedly cropping up these days is "spiritual"), there is the problem of violence done to the text: "Naturalistic" descriptions of sex and violence are invariably removed, as are derogatory remarks about the U.S.S.R. Socialist Realism, adept at seizing on dissident material (so abundant in postwar American fiction), proves woefully simplistic when dealing with novels whose content derives its meaning from style and form.

Thus, Vera Panova grapples briefly with the symbolism in *The Catcher in the Rye* (a best-selling novel in Russia since 1960), but as its meaning eludes her, she moralizes over its boy-hero, Holden, "a prisoner of this world . . . unaware that the world can and should be changed."

The Southern writer, passionately turning upon his aristocratic past, upon "the original sin of American history—slavery," interests the Soviet critic so long as he doesn't become too "literary" or "metaphysical" (both dirty words). Writing of *Set This House on Fire,* Mikhail Landor chides Styron for "introducing a somewhat anemic French superstructure" on a "full-blooded" Southern novel. Another critic, P. V. Palievsky, unable to find a purpose for Faulkner's experimental style in *The Sound and the Fury,* downgrades this work while extolling Faulkner's lesser later novels involving the evil, "capitalistic" Snopeses. How little Faulkner's real intent is understood may be seen by the critic's naïve comparison of the Southern author with the Russian Sholokhov: while the latter anticipates "revolutionary reconstruction," Faulkner "offered no more than he could offer—the old human values."

Not surprisingly, the Soviet critic is quick to respond to a title like Updike's *The Centaur* (translated in 1965). "Centaur novels" proves a handy tag to describe works in which the material and spiritual aspects of American life clash and remain unresolved. Countering Lionel Trilling's and David Riesman's "conformist fantasies," Landor shows how a writer like Updike asks basic questions, "awakening a society which is mesmerized by material comforts." For the same reason, Saul Bellow gets his share of praise, though his intellectual hero, Herzog, is faulted as only a pseudo-nonconformist, one crippled by the absence of "clear ideas." "The Marxist method," the critic concludes, "could free [these writers] from metaphysics."

If Bellow's raucous humor and quiet irony are only faintly heard in this long essay, the highly charged dichotomy of Mailer's prose remains all but inaudible on some remote frequency. The Soviet idea of man as a conditioned being at the mercy of social laws confronts uncomfortably the democratic notion of man as a complex being resisting his own false dreams and self-delusions. Mailer's critic, Nikolyukin, finds it hard to reconcile the anti-war novelist of yore who preached against American fascism and the more recent author of *An American Dream,* with its "cruel existentialist hero." Eclecticism in the Soviet lexicon can only spell failure; in Mailer's vocabulary it is a major defense against closed systems of thought.

After a heavy dose of ideological criticism, there is a new pleasure to be derived from the free-wheeling, paradoxical stance of a Mailer, however flawed his art. Like most of the novelists discussed, he is ever open to "change"—but not the purposeful, predetermined "change" prescribed by a system already deemed "perfect." The "change" he and other American novelists seek remains undefined and dependent, ultimately, on a personal conversion.

1973

The Charmed Circle:
The Irish Writers

The next best thing to hearing a literary Irishman talk is reading him talking: without the physical presence, we are robbed of the cadence and inflection (Whoever said that all speech is prose?), the intense joviality that punctuates a never-ending spiral of opinion, and what can only be described as a demonic gaze, full of hints of more to come. But the talk has other qualities that cold print cannot destroy: a constant shower of imagery, unfailing humor (never really black)—and always a contagious delight in the vagaries of human personality. It is gossip with the highest of motives: to expose the individual's essence, what sets him apart from the crowd.

The reader who picks up *Irish Literary Portraits,* a collection of spontaneous interviews, will find himself straightway in this charmed circle where, in addition, a treat lies in store for those who respond to the ambiguities of character. However deeply our impressions of the Irish writers have been firmed by Richard Ellmann, Harold Bloom, Denis Donoghue, Horace Gregory, etc., we cannot fully appreciate the multifacetedness of Yeats, Joyce, Shaw and their Dublin contemporaries until we have seen them through one another's eyes. Lucky for us, that feat was made possible—at the eleventh hour—when an Irish poet-minister-broadcaster, W. R. Rodgers, ventured to dredge the memories of the last survivors of the Irish Literary Movement.

In an ingenious series that ran on the British Broadcasting Corporation's Third Programme from 1949 to 1966, he interviewed such prominent elder statesmen (many since dead) as St. John Gogarty, Sean O'Casey, St. John Ervine, Austin Clarke, Sean O'Faolain, as well as family members and old flames of the writers discussed, newspaper editors, headwaiters and even veterans of the Easter Uprising, who derived so much of their national fervor from the Movement. Having recorded the witnesses separately and added his own useful commentary, Mr. Rodgers pulled the tapes together to provide, in each case, a kind of collage.

Mr. Rodgers called these "conversations" "studies in relationship," and warned his listeners that "truth is not the whole of life or facts the whole of truth." The truth, in retrospect, is most often exactly the sum of the contradictions—with wispy pieces sliding out of the larger design. Take Yeats. Uppermost in O'Faolain's recollection is the "mask," the pose (cane, flowing tie, long hair) that came between the poet and his "natural self." But a younger contemporary, Frank O'Connor, observed "a peculiar sort of innocence" in Yeats appropriate to a romantic poet. The two writers dispute whether or not a poet "in search of the reality of time and place" should frequent pubs (Yeats didn't) or flaunt bow ties (Dublin poets did). And while a curiously unromantic Mrs. McBride (Maud Gonne) testifies that he was "wonderful at a committee meeting," a Dublin scholar, Dr. Best, elaborates on Yeats's way of "being always on a higher plane."

Yeats's towering figure is the target throughout the interviews of irreverent, if unmalicious, downgrading. He eludes the Dubliners' sense of propriety, their need to be constantly gregarious and visible.

The author of *Ulysses,* on the other hand, is extolled for his bonhomie—with even the arrogant pose of the young artist in white yachting cap and white canvas shoes, peddling his own poems, seen only as a sign of his "curious sense of his own powers." Two Joyce sisters testify that he was religious; a headwaiter at Fouquet's remembers that he drank only moderately, gave big tips and copies of his new books. Gogarty offers vivid glimpses of Joyce's childhood poverty, while Frank Budgen recalls the "boyish" capers that lasted well into Joyce's maturity. "I don't think he liked women," is the impression of a Dublin friend. "He was frightened of them." All agree he was a loyal husband, devoted family man. As these and many other views are superimposed, an unbohemian Joyce emerges. We sense the separation of the artist and the man and know that the end of literary romanticism has come.

With Shaw, the man behind the self-created myth takes the stage. "When you consider the life," says Denis Johnston, "his knickerbockers and his vegetables, his Fabian pamphlets and his delicate fuss over actresses . . . none of it does justice to the Shaw inside." Except for the few neighbors who speak of the little-known early family life, the talk remains on an abstract level, with professions of his great kindness, his callousness, his emotional blocks, etc., bringing us no closer to the inner Shaw than Yeats's caustic view of him as "a smiling sewing machine." Fun as they are to read, these interviews are self-defeating, for as Mr. Rodgers aptly hints, Shaw is best observed in his plays. The man's depth flowed into his art and remained there.

Mostly it is the pub man's hearty exchange of oft-told tales that fills out the portraits of the lesser figures. One such concerns Gogarty's miraculous escape from his political captors and his midnight swim in the Liffey—told with all those native flights of fancy. Joyce's model for Buck Mulligan, Gogarty, was indeed larger than life; a poet, playwright, wit, athlete, surgeon and senator whose conversational feats were second to none. As one might have expected, he was put off by George Moore's epicureanism and couldn't resist making fun of that fastidious man's many mundane irritations.

Most steeped in legend is the talk about Synge and AE. The story of that explosive first production of *Playboy of the Western World* must have become endlessly refined in the telling. " 'This is the best thing that ever happened in my life,' " Yeats is reported to have said, "with the gleam of battle in his eye." There seemed little left to say about Synge after that. In some ways, the gentle, high-minded AE—whom O'Connor calls "the father of three generations of Irish poets"—never becomes more than an echo of hero worship (someone *must* be writing a biography of him). His "radiance," his devotion to the common good and to individuals alike is a tale that is endlessly spun. The man who designed the banner of the plough and the stars (symbol of the Irish Citizen Army) was the most lovable Dubliner of all, rising above his city's provincialism. Avoiding expatriation until the end of his life, AE could remain more "whole" than Yeats, Joyce or Shaw.

1973

PART FOUR

The Decline
of "Mass Markets"

Malcolm Bradbury, in *The Social Context of Modern English Literature,* examines an aspect of the literary scene that for all its importance has received little attention: the writer's changing relationship to his audience and the transformations it effects on both his art and his career. His focus is on the English scene, but the portrait he paints of the modern English writer as a thwarted and threatened independent spirit has implications for American writers as well.

Taking a more sociological approach than John Gross in *The Rise and Fall of the Man of Letters,* Mr. Bradbury traces the progress of the "serious" creative writer in this century from semi-dilettante and coterie writer, partially subsidized by private income and patronage, to modern technocrat writer, all but fully supported by "the large media and services." Economically speaking, the path has been anything but smooth, for as the writer became a professional, earning his living by writing, his commitment to literature and to his individual vision invariably came into conflict with the whims and fashions of the marketplace. In England the conflict had special edge.

Literary tradition and a stratified society were the great stumbling blocks to a wider readership for the author. Where few gradations existed between high and low culture—as was the case early in the century—a simultaneous appeal to both was hardly possible. A writer like Shaw or D. H. Lawrence might speak (as both did) for the middle class and even the working class in his novels or plays, but by virtue of his literary language and sensibility he would be only a little more widely read than an experimental writer like Joyce, seeking an underground reputation abroad, or a writer in the Virginia Woolf mold, opting for an income of £500 and a room of one's own. We think today of Shaw, Bennett, Wells and Orwell as widely successful writers of their day, but actually their independence as creative writers hinged on their extensive journalistic output both during and after their long apprenticeships.

In a sense, as Mr. Bradbury suggests, the Angry Young Men (Amis, Osborne, Wain, Braine, etc.) were the first generation of English writers to have a truly representative reading public—their uneasy class-consciousness reflecting the total breakdown of class in the postwar years. But their rebellion, directed at society at large, involved flight from a self-image of "innocence" as well as from Grub Street, and after the first shock of their rage wore off, the public grew bored with their soul-searchings. As independent writers (and they were not, of course, the only ones) they faced a choice between a return to bohemianism and a job with which to supplement their meager incomes from fiction writing. Since fewer little presses and literary journals could now be counted on to support even a bohemian existence, large numbers of writers turned to teaching, advertising or journalism, sacrificing their creative work when these fields could no longer remain sidelines. It is not a new story—except for what follows.

The startling part of Mr. Bradbury's report is the part that projects into the future. With something of Marshall McLuhan's transcendent faith in the technocratic society, he sees in the development of the popular media—television and film—the final reconciliation of the English writer and his elusive wider audience. Apparently the British media have largely avoided the heavily commercial and monolithic structure of the American equivalents, and the security they offer is only one of their many attractions for the new writer. What matters, as Mr. Bradbury sees it, is that the writer has become "a marketable commodity" in an area still novel and changing enough to welcome new ideas. Yet he admits that the media minimize individual achievements: innovations no longer emerge from a writer's personal vision but from a combination of technological advances in which the engineer's role is at least as important as the writer's! This latest image of the English writer as team-worker is hard indeed to reconcile with the free spirit of his traditional stamp.

The American writer's experience with his audience has in a way been the reverse of the English writer's. With no strict barriers of class to surmount and a much more flexible literary culture, he has been able from the start to command a wider spectrum of readership. What he has had to buck in an open society, as Malcolm Cowley has pointed out in *The Literary Situation,* is the rapid changes in literary climate (the "bohemian" of the twenties, the "proletarian" of the thirties, etc.) largely effected by the nation's economy or general mood. The wider the writer's appeal, the easier becomes the adjustment. In recent years a perfect example of this kind of writer has been Norman Mailer, his sharp antennae reaching out to a mass public, often only in ironic recognition.

Regional, educational and ethnic differences aside, social fluidity has made mass readership possible—indeed inevitable—in this country. The best seller as an institution is an American development, and it remains an American ideal, creating a hard division between the commercial and the noncommercial writer, with the latter dropping out when the going gets tough. Cowley's startling report in 1958 (a year of general affluence) read: "The average income of the writer from writing books is below the average earnings of Southern mill hands and not much above those of cotton sharecroppers."

With more books being published and read today than ever before, certainly the writer of *popular* books is better off than he has been in the past, but for the young creative writer making his way into the profession, the realization that success on a large scale is virtually the only success possible must be disheartening if not frustrating. With the cost of book production ever on the rise, fewer risks can be taken; the quiet writer must defer to the shocking and outrageous. Nor is it altogether reassuring to be told by an industry spokesman that publishing continues to be a booming business. Booming to whom? Certainly not to the fiction writer whose royalties remain incredibly out of line with an industry whose annual profit exceeds three billion dollars. Moreover, in the pursuit of standard business economics, the publisher may well lose interest in the *development* of an individual writer, since the apprenticeship stage is usually a losing one.

Yet for the serious American writer not interested in alternatives to publishing (and there is little noncommercial television or film to turn to), the search for an authentic audience continues. And if we are reading the signs right, the time may have come for a shift in emphasis. Despite the imposing presence of big-business con-glomerates on the publishing scene (RCA, CBS, ITT, etc.), there ap-pears to be a decentralizing tendency, a growing awareness that not *all* books (and this includes novels, poems, stories) need to be channeled to a mass market, but that most books would in fact profit by being directed to a more particularized one. Though personal publishing in this country never really lapsed (never having reached the elitist im-passe of the English scene), there has been a steady increase in the 1970s of small and independent houses, both in New York and out-side, publishing books that are reviewed and advertised nationally. Some have announced themselves simply as "cultural enterprises," without indicating preferences; others have stated their exclusive con-cerns, with large numbers of them taking up minority and ethnic prob-lems not dealt with elsewhere. None has yet uncovered great literary talent, and some observers contend that these small firms will not long remain small, nor in expanding will outgrow their second-rate status. Yet the fact that they are not exploiting the talentless in the manner of erstwhile vanity presses speaks in their favor. Even at this date their presence may be viewed as a reflection of a general tendency in the country at large away from the standard, the established, the whole-sale product.

An article published in the *Columbia Journalism Review*, "Can *Life* and *Look* Survive?" points out that even mass-audience magazines no longer make their main focus the mass-ness of their audience. (*Look* and *Life* have never been replaced.) If large-city newspapers are shutting down, suburban papers are thriving, just as local boutiques are competing with the department stores.

The fact is that there is no single emblematic image of America any more, no Babbitts and Mrs. Bridges. The rebels live side by side with the silent majority in an amalgamated America where, as the phrase goes, people "do their own thing," where as de Tocqueville observed, "the principle of equality naturally divides the American into a multitude of small private circles." These divisions "by small invisible threads" are the individual's safeguard against being "carried away against his will in a crowd." And indeed a faceless crowd asserting its amorphous will on the individual can be as lastingly destructive of a culture as an elitist minority imposing its mandarin ideals on a viable and changing society.

1973

The Lowly State
of Book Reviewing

I n 1959, critic Elizabeth Hardwick created a small sensation by
writing an article in *Harper's* on "The Decline of Book Reviewing." By announcing that "Sunday morning with the Book
Reviews [meaning the *New York Times* and the late *Herald Tribune*] is
often a dismal experience," she not only caused heads to topple but
inspired the idea for a new book review designed to correct this unhappy situation—namely, the *New York Review of Books,* which began
publication in 1963 during the extended New York newspaper strike.

Some nine years deeper into the age of mass electronic media, I
have no illusion about creating a similar sensation by reporting, in
1968, on the state of book reviewing *outside* New York. Miss Hardwick's tirade against soupy, innocuous reviewing was directed ex-
clusively at the New York scene. She was attacking the sources of
power: the *New York Times Book Review,* with its then circulation of
1,506,000;* the *Herald Tribune,* dead since 1966; and the *Saturday
Review* (circulation then 491,000). To find out what existed apart
from these powers, I decided to look out-of-town.

---

*The *Book Review*'s circulation is now over four million.

Statistics alone told part of the story. I discovered that outside New York City there were seventeen large-circulation Sunday newspapers that carried Sunday book sections—most often on a single page, tucked into a general entertainment section. There were only two supplements comparable in scope to that of the *Times: Book World,* shared by the *Washington Post* and the *Chicago Tribune,* and the even newer *Book Week,* in the *Chicago Sun-Times.*

Some papers, like the *Oregonian* of Portland (circulation 398,000), had no separate book page but reviewed books on politics or regional subjects on editorial pages. In the case of the Portland Sunday *Telegram,* Maine's largest paper (circulation 107,000), books were reviewed weekly only in summer, and biweekly and trimonthly in winter—the logic being, I suppose, that book reviews are for tourists! Some, like the Sunday *Detroit Free Press* (580,000) found a whole page too much for books and added a column on art on the same page.

I made a list of two dozen representative newspapers of varying Sunday circulations, ranging from the *Los Angeles Times*'s 970,000 to the *Providence Journal*'s 205,000. I wrote to their book editors for sample pages and brief reports on their methods of operation.

The response was quick and warm. With avid curiosity, I attacked the reading of a stack of the book pages submitted. All too soon my interest turned to disbelief and dismay as I observed how little space there was for reviewing, how poorly the reviews were displayed, how sloppy the editing often was, how incredible the choice of books reviewed—all this in newspapers that had circulations in the hundreds of thousands.

It was hard to avoid concluding that book reviewing on many newspapers was to all practical purposes the lowliest form of journalism (certainly in terms of compensation) and the editorship of a book section fell into the category of unsung heroism!

The reasons for this were multifarious and, understandably, essentially economic. Presumably there were not so many book readers outside New York (even in Boston, Chicago, San Francisco and

Philadelphia) and certainly far too few bookstores. The publishing industry, moreover, was centered in New York. But beyond these deterrents, book reviewing by its very nature presented a difficult problem to newspapers. It was a luxury. Where the circulation was large, there was the problem of adjusting a non-mass product (for how many best sellers are there, after all?) to a mass medium, the newspaper. And for the smaller newspapers, there was the financial hitch: you need advertising to make space for reviews, and publishers were reluctant to spend for ads outside New York.

Newspapers have tried to solve their book-page problems variously. To make books palatable to mass audiences, book news is emphasized over reviews. Critical judgment is abrogated, and in its place we are likely to be given material prepared by a publicity writer. On papers with small budgets, a syndicated column presenting the views of a single man may take the place of diverse bylines. This man's views are repeated in dozens of papers throughout the country. Finally, no one has yet been able to discover how to find qualified reviewers for books in special fields when all one can afford to pay a reviewer is $15 or less, or sometimes nothing at all! Under the circumstances, it is a wonder that we have the numerous instances of excellence that exist. Those I will discuss later.

First, here is what my correspondents had to say about their jobs as book editors:

Book pages were frequently placed in the hands of general reporters and editorial writers with some literary background who were also engaged in other work on the newspaper. Theirs was often a labor of love, to which, in the larger cities, a few fringe benefits were attached. As one editor put it: "There are the extracurricular activities, such as getting authors to come for book and author luncheons, dinners, etc., prowling around bookstores to find out what books are going and which are not, yakking with publishers' sales representatives, and all that jolly, jolly bit." Occasionally the editor of a book page was a professor who came into the newspaper office once or twice a week; one was a professor of philosophy at the University of Cincinnati, and another taught English literature at Los

Angeles State College. Another, like the book editor of the *Chattanooga Times,* was a librarian. ("I am not at the *Times* frequently," this editor wrote me in apology for his late answer.) Or one may have been, as in the case of the editor at the *Hartford Courant,* a retired schoolteacher.

An editor from a newspaper in the Northwest with a circulation of 276,000 wrote:

> As you can see, I am given ten tabloid columns to fill each week. I have been doing this for twenty-five years, and all, believe me, in my spare time. I put in a full day as a news editor on our evening editions. Mostly I write the pages myself, since I have no budget for paying reviewers. Sometimes I use a *Times Service* review, and occasionally someone will do a particular review just for the book. Except in politics, I am given wide latitude with my weekly column and often write on non-literary subjects, ranging from hunting and fishing to rose gardening and redecorating our home.

Harriet Doar, the enterprising and talented book editor of a much smaller Southern paper, the *Charlotte Observer,* reported that she received 3,000 books a year, of which only ten percent were reviewed. Here are telling passages from her report:

> I am surprised and touched at the writers [she named Lillian Smith and Harry Golden] who will take time to review since we cannot pay them anything. . . . We have a new university branch here, and the professors are good about reviewing. Housewives are often good, particularly those who do a little writing. . . . I would like to have more reviews of books dealing with international problems, but I find these hardest to get done well. Those with specialized knowledge want to go on forever, and I don't feel competent enough to cut and edit those properly.

The previously mentioned editor who was going to all those jolly parties also had his headaches, and he wrote:

> Newspapers would have better book coverage if they could get more book advertising and vice versa. Your *New York Times* is not only villainous but a really malicious influence on American journalism in this respect. Rates for *Book Review* are so high and the publishers are so impressed to see their ads there that the *Times* consumes most advertising budgets before they can be placed elsewhere.

Absence of space, of staff, of advertising, of adequate reviewers—these were the major complaints.

And there were other problems. The first thing to catch your eye was the conglomeration of books reviewed. While some papers reviewed a major book like Truman Capote's *In Cold Blood* promptly, most of them reviewed books that came out perhaps three months earlier and in 500 words or fewer. Considering the meagerness of space, one wondered that so much space was given to third-rate novels, to such miscellany as books on yoga, wine drinking, or Celtic myths, or how-to books. If on occasion a literary title or an important book on world affairs sneaked in, it was almost swallowed up.

This choice, it must be pointed out, was not completely the editor's. It was partly dictated by the books that publishers were willing to send him. Since they rarely advertised their books in these newspapers, publishers were reluctant to send all their best titles and thus made arbitrary selections based on preconceived notions of what would sell in St. Louis, Omaha or Dallas. As for the time lag, whereas the *New York Times* receives its books at least six weeks before publication, the out-of-town papers often received their copies *after* the book had been published.

Book publishers, moreover, showed little regard for special regional interests. The book editor of the *Dallas Times Herald* wrote:

> Publishers never seem to realize that a Texas news-
> paper is interested in all Texas items. . . . My chief com-
> plaint is that the book industry is so confined to the isle
> of Manhattan.

To return to the book pages. Most of them, as mentioned earlier,
consisted of a single page, usually tucked into the final portions of the
entertainment section. (The *Boston Traveler* called it "Show Guide.")
In a few instances, like the *Los Angeles Times* and the *San Francisco
Chronicle,* the reviews were spaced over a few pages and appeared
alongside art and music notes or large movie ads. Generally there was
a columnist, and although he titled his column something like "The
World of Books," books merely provided an excuse for airing views
that were ultimately not very literary. Sometimes, he might review a
book simply because it catered to a special taste or interest of the columnist, or sometimes, possibly, because the author of the book was a
friend. The kind of columnist who gets around would often interrupt
his comments on the book at hand with such asides as "at lunch the
other day the author of this book told me . . . ," which didn't leave
much room for critical comment.

The reviewing, at its worst, was catastrophic—mere puffs based on
publicity releases, but less well written and edited. Even when the
reviewers were not identified as housewives (in some cases their ad-
dresses were given—so the author could protest?), even when the
reviews were by academics, professionals, the critical caliber was very
low, with the emphasis placed less on the book's meaning or art than
on its author. It would seem that most usually the author with a striking personality or reputation got the most attention. Thus, even with a
thinker like Paul Tillich (if his book was reviewed at all), what was
emphasized was Tillich the man and his life, rather than Tillich's
philosophy.

Perhaps what was finally most disheartening was the feeling one
got that books were regarded as a mere commodity. When a frivolous
book by Patrick Dennis (author of *Auntie Mame*) was given equal

space with a Cambridge historian's biography of the Earl of Southampton, one wondered if the juxtaposition of these reviews was dictated by anything aside from the fact that the Earl and Mr. Dennis sported similar beards!

Yet I do not want to leave the impression that all is hopeless. Quite the contrary. Editors are generally aware of shortcomings and eager to do something about them. There is growing recognition that reviewing must be raised to a professional level, and more and more academic people and creative writers are being used as reviewers. Finally, one can single out at least half a dozen editors who are doing outstanding work—some of them despite limited resources and inadequate compensation or recognition.

In the late 1960s, Thorpe Menn of the *Kansas City Star,* A. C. Greene of the *Dallas Times Herald,* Robert Cromie of the *Chicago Tribune,* and Robert Kirsch of the *Los Angeles Times* made a careful selection of material and reviewers, and tried to reflect literary trends with understanding, while themselves writing with authority. Edwin Tribble of the *Washington Star* edited a lively page, and there were others of varying degrees of success, such as the *Providence Journal, Detroit News, San Francisco Chronicle, Denver Post,* the *Christian Science Monitor,* the *Milwaukee Journal,* and the *National Observer.* Among smaller papers, the Riverside (California) *Press-Enterprise* ran a solid and literate section..

Still more hearteningly, one encountered on occasion fresh talents and provocative points of view. The writers often had little or no sacrosanct feeling about literary reputations and took slowly to literary vogues. This is how a reviewer in Kansas City approached Edmund Wilson:

> I recall reading with great pleasure many of Edward [oops!] Wilson's essays in "The Bit Between My Teeth" when they first appeared in *New Yorker* magazine, but they do not stand up well upon second reading. This collection of his pronouncements over the last 13 years

strikes me as long and rambling, unified by nothing but the author's increasing vanity and dogmatism. . . . Wilson is ungracefully aging into a victim of the too common American assumption that the whole world should get worked up over the crotchets of talented individuals. . . . he resembles in his latest work the resolutely independent grocer in a world of faceless supermarkets—a still admirable but somewhat obsolescent figure.

This not only is candid but is expressed in a colorful, individual manner. It would probably never have been published in New York. And from the same city recently came the best assessment of John O'Hara as a moralist that I have ever read.

And there was fearlessness. The *San Francisco Chronicle*'s critic, for instance, minced no words when writing about Capote's *In Cold Blood*. In a review as long as the one in the *New York Times Book Review,* Evan S. Connell, Jr., presented one of the most effective dissenting views on this book, his final verdict being that it was "as powerless and empty of ominous significance as a dead snake." When a book is being heralded on every side as a masterpiece and is earning the author a cool million, it takes courage to go out on a limb.

There are disadvantages to being away from the center of power. But there are important compensations, too:

1. Far from New York's promotional hullabaloo, there is less danger of drifting with the tide.

2. The style of writing can remain fresher because it is less at the mercy of professional editing, which can, and often does, destroy individuality of expression.

3. Because little in the way of personal power is at stake, it is easier to be dissenting and completely honest.

Book World, the new supplement in the *Washington Post* and the *Chicago Tribune,* by aiming to be "a national book review with a national outlook," may further tend to weaken the expression of diverse regional interests and opinions from which ultimately the richness of our culture derives. There is always danger in consolidation. But it should take some of the power away from New York—which is all to the good.

If we want to raise the quality of literary journalism in the country at large—and at the same time utilize all our creative and critical resources—we cannot, it seems to me, continue to center our attention on a single geographical area. Because New York is the publishing center, we have allowed it to dominate the literary scene. I think it is time to take a longer and larger look at the reviewing scene. Let us not flatter ourselves that as New Yorkers we lead the nation. Let us, instead, keep our ears cocked to hear what the rest of the nation is saying. It is an education we can use.

1968

Poets, Printers
and Pamphleteers

I f your receiver of "future shock" has not yet picked up the reverberations coming from the so-called underground presses
and their affiliates—some 2,000 independent small presses and
magazines—you've been missing one of the liveliest cultural
phenomena of our day. This most recent form of dissent from the
literary and publishing establishments has so rapidly gained ground it
is assuming the proportions of a movement comparable to the paper-
back revolution of the fifties. Though I had not missed the distant
rumblings (who does not know the *Feminist Press,* Ferlinghetti's *City
Lights,* the sublimely angry *The Smith?*), I came upon it full blast
early in July 1974 at the New York Book Fair. In a novel kind of experiment, some 250 representative presses of the "alternate publishing
culture" convened from all parts of the country to exhibit their
wares—and possibly to sell them. To their own surprise, about 10,000
people, including members of the publishing establishment, turned up
to look, buy and even applaud.

For three days several floors of the New York Cultural Center
teemed with counterculture groups (in typical attire), along with
doughty entrepreneurs of both sexes, Third World and *Feminist Press*

leaders, idealistic, smooth-browed editors from the provinces (flower children grown up?), specialists in poetry, social change, yoga, ecology, gay liberation, black literature, films—everything, in fact, you've ever wanted to write yourself and didn't know could get printed. Paper shortage? No one apparently had heard of it. Mind-boggling, this open floodgate of creativity flaunting its independence from a "monolithic publishing structure"! I have not stopped reading that insect print since, trying to catch up with an "industry" that has been building since the early sixties.

A quick flip through the little "mags" (casual and unpretentious) suggests that a whole new generation of writers has emerged that has never had that devastating impersonal "No" from the *Atlantic,* never contended with the editorial blue pencil, nor faced the frustrations of the author published by a major press and promptly abandoned to an amorphous "public" (often nonexistent). For this new breed of writers, the word "public" has indeed narrowed down to include only those readers it wants and expects to reach. Because small independent publishers are often also editors and editors are also writers, there's harmony of a sort here unknown to trade publishers locked in the paraphernalia of publicity, advertising and the regular issuance of royalty statements. Not without its own paraphernalia, cooperative and collective publishing has established a scene of its own, with its own avant-garde.

That earlier group of rebels—the Pounds, Eliots and Joyces—had their literary "angels" who helped keep their independence alive. But the publishers and magazines that took them on had no risk insurance in the form of grants from the National Endowment for the Arts or the Coordinating Council of Little Magazines, which have come along since. No doubt the grants would have been welcomed. One wonders, though, if that other generation would have understood the com-munal feeling that led to the formation in 1968 of the Committee of Small Magazine Editors and Publishers, and if it would have approved of COSMEP's intricate schemes and programs for wider distribution.

But the analogy cannot be pressed. Literature is only one of the many concerns of the independent presses. Private ownership of the means of production has opened up new possibilities for the socially oriented writer eager to take up minority causes, particularly the unpopular ones trade publishers reject. With quick and easy access to print and a network of nationwide readership based on shared ideas and ideals, poet and reformer have turned into ardent pamphleteers. In the age of Xerox, letterpress and offset printing, wielders of the word machines can no more be stopped than the sorcerer's apprentice!

With their unlikely names (*Unmuzzled Ox, Mulch, Box 749 Magazine*), their casual mixture of genres, their reliance on middlebrow language and expression, the little "mags" are eye-catching (if not always absorbing) in a way that the academia-sponsored ones could never be. From Brooklyn to Berkeley, they represent a staggering regional range that could taunt if not threaten the Eastern Literary Establishment. One cannot but be impressed (sometimes enchanted) by the efforts and dedication of individual presses and editors: David Godine (the Boston publisher of rare elegance); Elizabeth Fisher's pioneering feminist magazine *Aphra; Extensions,* with its excellent translations; Bill Henderson's jaunty *Pushcart Press* (in Yonkers). But for every astutely edited magazine, like Martin Tucker's *Confrontations,* there are, unluckily, three or four that reek of phoniness and self-indulgence, undercutting the press freedom they advocate. One journal, professing "no limitation as to contents and style except common sense and conciseness," goes on to advocate, in its editorial, "surrender to our intuition as our best and most reliable source of guidance."

In the absence of traditional standards and direction, what one deplores most is an indifference to words beyond their common exchange value—even in the poetry. Here are the true heirs of John Brockman, whose 1971 book *Afterwords* proclaimed that "language is becoming obsolete." Brockman's creed that writers must immerse themselves in the "Pure Out There," to tune in on "the cosmos," finds its echo in much that gets printed under the guise of "literary idealism."

There is a great deal of talk these days in alternate publishing circles about the need to break through the "controls" of distribution channels. So far there's been wisdom in their search for authentic audiences. But their efforts to widen their markets may involve a backward look for a change—to the old experimenters who renounced commercialism without permanently alienating themselves from the cultural mainstream.

1974

They Gambled on Genius

It was time somebody set the record straight and showed how American expatriates transformed literary Paris in the nineteen twenties and thirties, and not the other way around. Too many memoirs of that period have played up the impact of the international scene on "the lost generation" of American writers, while barely acknowledging that it was a group of talented, plucky Americans who got the modernist movement (begun in France and England) off the ground. Though Hugh Ford's chunky, awkwardly assembled chronicle *Published in Paris* includes British expatriates as well, it is the

Americans who loom larger as promoters of the new literature. Dealing with their individual careers in separate chapters, Mr. Ford makes only fitful stabs at the nostalgia of "being geniuses together." He unfolds, instead, a piquant panorama of an era in publishing when editors, critics and even booksellers gambled on genius before it knew its strength and found its audience.

Paris, the eternal playground, was that and more to the young "exiles": It was a place to experience books as literature and not a commodity to be consumed like the daily newspaper by all. For some, there was a kind of snobbery in being able to print one's own work in small, elegant editions marked "not for sale." Not that commercial publishing was entirely scorned. While reading one another's works, they hoped to be noticed by impassioned, author-watching critics (Ezra Pound, Edmund Wilson, Ford Madox Ford) and subsequently by trade publishers who would buy their Paris editions. Taking their cue from Picasso, who said, "You paint not what you see but what you know is there," they dreamed their private dreams and helped one another to success.

Sylvia Beach, the Princeton pastor's daughter who opened her Shakespeare and Company bookshop on the Left Bank in 1919, was not herself a writer; she was not even an editor when destiny sent the controversial James Joyce to her doorstep. A literary dilettante with modest means, she cultivated the avant-garde in search of clients for her shop. But empathy for the writer with a mission turned her overnight into the publisher of the era's most explosive book, *Ulysses*. With a fine sense of the absurd and more details than we have had before, Mr. Ford lingers on the long and arduous stages through which this incongruous team labored to bring forth a masterpiece.

The element of chance was never absent from the makeshift transactions of those who published in Paris. But, within limits, there was also deliberate planning. From his home base at Miss Beach's bookshop (and also the cafés of Paris), Robert McAlmon made all the right connections as he seesawed between pursuit of his own literary ambitions and a fanatical urge to advance an American literature grounded in "direct experience with life." Money from a rich father-in-law (his wife was the English writer Bryher) enabled him to start the Contact Publishing Company, which (together with Three Mountains Press) helped start off the careers of dozens of British and American writers, among them Ernest Hemingway and William Carlos Williams. Neither his own rejections nor the prevailing "European" influences of T. S. Eliot and Pound deterred him from publishing one of the most labyrinthine works in the English language, Gertrude Stein's *The Making of Americans.*

Though a few of the presses had special axes to grind, personal publishing in Paris was chiefly stirred by a revolutionary zeal to extend the possibilities of language and examine newfound interior worlds. At Three Mountains Press, Bill Bird captured the collectors' market with handset editions in original typography; he published Pound's *Cantos* and *Indiscretions* and Mr. McAlmon's stories of homosexuals. Edward Titus, bibliophile and husband of Helena Rubinstein, gambled on the banned and pirated *Lady Chatterley's Lover* (after Miss Beach had turned it down) and introduced the surrealist poets in English. Harry and Caresse Crosby's Black Sun Press subsidized Hart Crane through five years of writing *The Bridge,* and Gertrude Stein and Anaïs Nin set up their own presses to publish their unmarketable, sophisticated works. At the Hours Press, the dedicated, energetic Nancy Cunard encouraged the growing taste for bizarre and unorthodox works, publishing among others the fledgling Samuel Beckett. And, anticipating the holocaust in 1939, Michael Frankel at Carrefour collaborated with Henry Miller on a "dialogue on death" titled *Hamlet.*

Except for Jack Kahane of Obelisk Press (who cashed in on underground books after he published Mr. Miller's *Tropic of Cancer*), the small press owners in Paris weighed immaterial success against financial loss and found the loss less important. Their growing interest in shocking, "decadent" subjects was part of their rebellion against glib and commonplace truths and was not intended to exploit the lower instincts. The self-transcending visions of Harry Crosby (who mysteriously took his life at thirty-one) proved an irresistible magnet to writers who shared his Janus-faced demon. Fixed as symbols of "the lost generation," the Crosbys have remained elusive presences in the diaries of their contemporaries. Now we see that they most certainly had substance: Among the significant modernist works they published from 1925 to 1931 (with Caresse's going on well into the thirties) were Harry's own remarkable diaries, which remain "undiscovered."

Harry Crosby's frenzied life (like Mr. McAlmon's) is told in tantalizing bits and pieces. Mr. Ford's relentless researches lead us in too many different directions at once, mixing, chaotically sometimes, titles, plots, anecdotes and characterizations. Even in its useful bibliography of publications, there is a general lack of scholarly precision. This is too bad, for greater care in the writing and a more personal response would have made this book an impressive, much-needed rejoinder.

1975

AFTERWORD

Around and about the year 1964 a drastic change took place on the American literary scene. When both Faulkner and Hemingway died, traditional links with a humanistic past were abruptly severed. An atmosphere of political and social unrest began to leave its imprint on a newly emerging generation of writers. The Kennedy assassination, followed by a series of violently staged protests and demonstrations throughout the country, impelled these writers to turn dramatically away from the native American stance of optimism. As the specter of the American Dream all but vanished, the inclination to nurture despair reached such large proportions that by the end of the decade the apocalypse seemed very near at hand indeed.

At the same time, that extraordinarily talented group of postwar writers, those humanists in the existential vein—Norman Mailer, Saul Bellow, J. D. Salinger, Carson McCullers, Eudora Welty, Vladimir Nabokov, among others—reached their apex. Though they had proved a durable lot, with no tragic cop-outs or suicides, hard times lay ahead for them. McCullers and Kerouac succumbed to illness; Salinger went into hiding, hoping to emerge with a magnum opus; McCarthy, Baldwin, Styron and Nabokov exiled themselves in Europe for nonpolitical reasons; others, like Jean Stafford, Wright Morris and James Purdy, held on by the skin of their teeth, waiting—it seemed—for a change in the literary climate that would not come. Eudora Welty, Bernard Malamud, Herbert Gold and John Updike, all short-story writers basically, learned to accommodate to the public taste for longer fiction. (Miss Welty happily adapted the story form to the episodic novel.) At times their talents seemed barely to escape being straitjacketed. For others, popularity was achieved at the expense of an initial artistic vision. Updike, by writing too often and too profusely, lost the poetically serene and piquant quality of his early fiction. And though one came to admire the essayist-philosopher Saul Bellow of *Mr. Sammler's Planet* (a work worthy of his stature as a Nobel Prize winner), one missed the exuberant, earthy characters that had caused his earlier novels to overflow with life. Mailer remained our weathervane, turning in all directions, his brilliant mind faltering only before the art of fiction. Like Welty, Nabokov retained the original stamp of his genius, though, unlike her, he grew more and more esoteric, less read than collected.

Why did this generously endowed group of writers so soon relinquish their preeminence on the literary scene? One reason, I suggest, stemmed from the limitations that our socioeconomic situation began to place on the imaginative writer in the 1960s. To make a living, the fiction writer had to seek an increasingly wider audience. At the same time, as book publishing became more costly (manufacturing and production costs have increased substantially in recent years), publishers were less willing to take on manuscripts of limited or special appeal. To survive, the writer of fiction learned to keep up with literary trends and fashions (not necessarily always congenial to his taste and talent), with the result that his natural growth was inhibited. In order to remain in the limelight, the writer found that he was simply repeating himself or merely skimming the surface of contemporary innovations.

Beyond the survival factor, there was a self-inflicted form of restraint: the feeling of futility brought about by a world where a galloping technology and automation diminish the human capacity to respond to works of art. To capture readers for whom time was increasingly fragmented and precisely measured in Eliot's proverbial coffee spoons, became no small feat. The writer now had to shock readers to attention, and often to titillate and outrage them.

For the energetic writers of the sixties and seventies, such problems seem less restrictive, for their talents adjust more easily to prevailing circumstances. With their feet on neutral ground (where neither great new dreams are dreamed nor old ones mourned), they are the generation of the Cold War in American fiction. Unhappy with the world as they find it, but reluctant (or unable) to engage in a struggle that might destroy the good with the bad, they succeed best when they dilute their outrage with a measure of grim laughter. These "black humorists," as they have come to be known, have learned to exploit their sense of futility, locking their fears and hallucinations in a fantasy world that mimics the irrelevancies of "real" life.

Not committed, as were Sartre and Camus, to an explication of the metaphysical contours of our lives, writers like Heller, Vonnegut, Barth, Burroughs and Didion seek only to render the chaotic absurdity of modern life in terms that can be directly comprehended. (How easy their task of shocking readers to attention!) At the center of the stage is no longer the hero or anti-hero, or even a particular aspect of contemporary society, but an overpowering, faceless Society within which the individual is virtually lost. Closely controlled in form if not in other aspects of literary technique, their novels often read like extended metaphors, which by repetition achieve the effect of a ballet, a *danse macabre.*

If one notes in their work traces of the expressionism of a Nathanael West or a Bertolt Brecht, it is because, like them, these black humorists are negators and distrustors of Utopias. But there is a pithy longing for stability behind the despair of a West or a Brecht—an unwillingness to accept the void—that is alien to the more disenchanted writer of our day. Irrational, irresponsible, outrageously irreverent, these latter-day satirists mock and desecrate many things, not least of all the common impulse to war against abuses. They are weary of all attempts to circumscribe the truth or lend order to the universe; frequently the offender for them is as vast and as unassailable as Civilization itself. All too rarely, if we except Vonnegut's early work, does the laughter in which they wallow bring about the cathartic release of true satire.

Because fiction itself has become an object of parody, many writers now deliberately avoid the accepted tenets of literary art. Two-dimensional characters, a series of disconnected incidents and a vague or monotonous narrative that repeats its simple statement ad infinitum—these and other characteristics are turning the novel form inside out, without at the same time contributing concretely to its reconstruction. At the ordinary entertainment level, the models most often followed are science fiction, pornography, and the Western. One could not begin to list the undistinguished titles (mostly by one-novel writers) published within the last fifteen years.

On a more literary level of achievement—apart from those novels already mentioned—is the work of the Western novelist and poet Richard Brautigan *(Trout Fishing in America, The Abortion* and *In Watermelon Sugar),* playful, anarchistic, improvised. There are also the highly touted inverted narratives of Donald Barthelme *(Snow White, City Life* and his most recent *The Dead Father* being perhaps his best)—surreal fragments of dislocated urban life steeped in the fairy-tale mode. And, most ambitious, the cryptic, futuristic works (one scarcely wants to call them novels) of Thomas Pynchon (with *Gravity's Rainbow* his most daring), which break ground in their application of the thermodynamic concept of "entropy" to modern life.

Very possibly a new form of the novel is in the making, one in which the attention will be riveted not to its psychological dimensions (so acutely probed by earlier postwar novelists), but to the forces which go into the making of those dimensions, shifting and altering our perception of human nature so that no fixed portrait of the individual becomes possible (as indeed has long been the case in modern painting).

But wherever these writers are leading us, one thing, one hopes, will remain unchanged: the novelist's awareness of the self as a thing apart from the circumstantial world. The nihilistic climate in which the novel has settled is tending to absorb the human component into the material world, and by so doing is diminishing our capacity to relate to fiction. If the novel cannot make us feel concern for ourselves, for others, for our larger fate as human beings, how can we expect it to retain its hold on us? The need now is for writers who can see through their dark laughter a purpose (however elusive) that makes the writing of imaginative fiction a valid occupation.

1977